The Paranormal Investigator's *Handbook*

The Paranormal Investigator's *Handbook*

Edited by
Valerie Hope &
Maurice Townsend

COLLINS & BROWN

First published in Great Britain in 1999 by
Collins & Brown Limited
London House
Great Eastern Wharf
Parkgate Road
London SW11 4NQ

Distributed in the United States and Canada by Sterling Publishing Co,
387 Park Avenue South, New York, NY 10016, USA

1 3 5 7 9 8 6 4 2

British Library Cataloguing-in-Publication Data:
A catalogue record for this title is available from the British Library.

ISBN 1-85585-703-0 (paperback)

Editorial Director: Sarah Hoggett
Editors: Katie Bent and Mary Lambert
Designer: Claire Graham

Reproduced by HBM Print, Singapore
Printed and bound by Dai Nippon, Hong Kong

CONTENTS

WHAT ARE ANOMALOUS PHENOMENA?

ROM THE BEGINNING OF TIME people have reported seeing strange phenomena that defied normal explanation. Centuries ago these were generally accepted as signs of the intervention of gods or spirits. With many cultures believing in an afterlife, a sighting of someone known to be dead would be seen as unusual, but not impossible, and definitely significant. When some odd coincidence occurred it would be regarded as a portent from the gods. Similarly, an unusual occurrence such as a sudden fall of fish from the sky would also be considered an important heavenly sign.

• THE SCIENTIFIC VIEW •

In recent centuries, people have used science as part of the philosophical framework to understand the world and the events that happen within it. One of the central ideas of science is that the theories that it presents can be tested by anyone at any time. For example, if an unknown professor makes claims that he can make a metal harder by adding a particular chemical, you do not have to take his word for it. You can read other research or studies on the principle, or even get another professor to do further tests to substantiate the theory. So science could be described as practical philosophy.

But where do anomalous phenomena fit into the scientific viewpoint? Basically they don't. They are given this name because the events that happen do not fit into existing theories. In some cases they seem to flatly contradict existing scientific theory. For this reason scientists often ignore or even attack seemingly inexplicable paranormal observations.

Because of the widespread acceptance of this scientific view today, when someone sees a ghost, many people will question the observation. It does not help that these are usually rare, unexpected events that are hardly ever recorded on film or electronically. It is, therefore, relatively easy for scientists to dismiss such reports. There is, however, a consistent record of such events occurring down the centuries. And since people have consistently reported the presence of ghosts and other phenomena up to modern times, it is difficult to argue that they have all been mistaken.

• TYPES OF ANOMALOUS PHENOMENA •

There are many different anomalous phenomena. The term covers all paranormal as well as some rare 'normal' phenomena. All that appears to connect them is the mystery of how they came about. Recently, however, more concrete connections have emerged between phenomena. For instance, many people who have seen unidentified flying objects (UFOs) are known to have witnessed other psychic happenings. Other people may start having such experiences after witnessing their first UFO encounter.

The main reason, however, why many disparate phenomena are linked together as a single subject is that people who might be interested in UFOs, for example, may also want to find out about ley lines or telepathy. This may not seem a very sound justification for treating these phenomena together, but they do need a similar method of investigation. And that is essentially what this book is about. It is concerned with how a paranormal investigator would go about collecting and analyzing information on anomalous or paranormal phenomena.

• UFO SIGHTING *Strangely-shaped clouds can account for some UFO reports.*

PSYCHIC PHENOMENA

These are the apparent abilities of humans (or indeed animals) to sense or influence their environment without using the normal senses. This type of phenomenon includes telepathy, psychokinesis, mediumship, apparitions, psychometry and unorthodox healing – such as the 'laying on of hands'.

Psychic phenomena are generally connected with people. They are usually either things that people can do, such as bend metal by gentle stroking, or things that are witnessed by people, such as ghosts. If the phenomenon is a person's

7

special ability, such as foretelling the future, then it can be tested in a scientific experiment. If it is something that is witnessed, then it may be possible to see it again if people go back to the same place and wait for a sufficiently long time. In the latter case, instruments can also be taken along to record the event so it can be studied in a reasonably scientific way.

EARTH MYSTERIES

The best known example of this study of phenomena tied to particular places is that of leys or ley lines. These are lines that are thought to join ancient monuments or prehistoric tracks. Archaeologists have always disputed that such alignments exist, but this has not stopped people covering maps in straight lines and continuing to look for them. Reports have been received of many unusual phenomena, such as lights, sounds, or strange feelings, that are associated with ancient sites. Some people claim to be able to sense where underground structures are (both at ancient sites and elsewhere) through dowsing. This is, perhaps, a psychic ability but it is extensively used in the study of Earth mysteries.

Detailed research into a particular area can be done over many years. This could involve cataloguing unusual phenomena in the area, dowsing, or looking through ancient records for hints of any paranormal experiences in the

• FALLING FISH
Fortean phe-
nomena include
such anomalies
as fish falling
from the sky.

past. Local legends can often relate to paranormal happenings. Such studies reveal that some places are more prone to anomalies than others. It is also possible to examine sites using scientific instruments to see if there is anything objectively different about them.

FORTEAN PHENOMENA

These are a varied collection of scientific curiosities such as falls of fish from the sky, out-of-place animals, for example crocodiles in the sewers of New York, weeping religious statues and crop circles.

Fortean phenomena are named after Charles Fort, who collected records of unusual events that scientists ignored because they just did not fit in with their theories. Fortean phenomena tend to 'just happen' and are often reported after the event. There is usually no reason to connect them with the presence of people or particular places as they are often just unusual natural curiosities. Investigating them is difficult, as they may be observed by only one or two people and leave no physical trace. This is the case, for example, when an out-of-place animal is sighted. Because they are very rare and unpredictable events, there is often very little point waiting for anything to happen again.

'... unusual aerial objects have been observed for centuries ...'

UFOLOGY

The most limited major subject within the anomaly field is that of unidentified flying objects (UFOs). Ufology, nevertheless, enjoys the highest media profile because of the widely held theory that UFOs are vehicles for visitors from other planets. In fact, unusual aerial objects have been observed for centuries and in the past were often seen as flying witches or gods. Even today, there are plenty of other theories to explain why UFOs exist, although none captures the public imagination so much as the extra-terrestrial hypothesis.

Usually UFOs are one-off events and they rarely leave any physical traces. For this reason, often the only way of studying them is to interview witnesses. As UFO sightings are rare events no one wants to wait in certain places for one to happen. However, there are particular geographical areas where sightings seem to be more prevalent.

• WHY INVESTIGATE ANOMALOUS PHENOMENA? •

If most scientists view anomalous phenomena with such scorn, why do people bother with them at all? It is precisely because scientists ignore them that fascinated amateurs want to fill the gap. There are some scientists who would like to investigate anomalous phenomena and there are even some who do – research is regularly carried out on ESP, for instance. But it is difficult to get grants for areas that are not well supported.

If an anomalous phenomenon can be shown to be undeniably real, it would have to be taken seriously by scientists. As we have seen, science is about things that can be demonstrated objectively. Once a phenomenon has been proved to exist, then theories that do not fit the new facts will have to be changed. It would cause what scientists call a paradigm shift. Many anomalous or paranormal phenomena hint at things that are well beyond current scientific thinking. To prove that they actually exist would therefore be a great achievement and well worth the paranormal investigator's time. Many of the phenomena represented in this book can be researched by a keen amateur. If you would like to take your investigations further, contact one of the organizations listed on page 144.

• HOW TO INVESTIGATE PARANORMAL EVENTS •

So, how do you start to investigate paranormal incidents? There are many possible methods to use. You can, for instance, take a belief-oriented view. In this approach you accept that a ghost, for instance, represents a 'returning spirit', trying to get in touch. There are indeed people who take just such an approach, viewing ghosts purely with this belief in mind. However, as we shall see (in Chapter 2, 'Hauntings') it is still being debated as to whether ghosts really are 'returning spirits'.

Another approach is to adopt a more sceptical attitude. Anomalous phenomena are seen as not being explicable in terms of current science, but requiring normal explanations. In other words, all such phenomena are viewed as being misinterpretations of naturally occurring events. It is often expressed as 'extraordinary claims demand extraordinary proof'. Unfortunately, this target can often seem to be just out of reach.

In fact, these approaches are similar in that they both presuppose something about the nature of the phenomena they seek to explain, which is generally not the way science works. If we are to truly explain these phenomena, the most sensible way forward would seem to be to study them without any initial prejudice. The investigator should follow where the facts lead, finding out if there is a consistent phenomenon to study and, if there is, explain what it is by using proven scientific methods. This neutral approach is followed by many leading researchers and is the one expressed in this book.

ELIMINATING NORMAL EXPLANATIONS

If it is reported to you that someone has seen a 'huge spaceship' hovering over their garden it might sound like a definitive anomalous phenomenon. But you might well find out on subsequent investigation that it was just a weather balloon seen through a cloud. Many reports, when carefully analysed, turn out to have 'normal' explanations. Clearly then, the first thing any investigator must do first is to check for mundane possibilities. Only once all the normal explanations have been successfully eliminated can the case be considered as one featuring anomalous phenomena.

'The investigator should follow where the facts lead ' ...

The first stage of any investigation, therefore, is to gather together all the facts. This can be done by interviewing witnesses, examining the site of the event and looking for any residues or effects that the phenomenon may have left (see also Chapter 1, 'Investigating'). What you need to look for will depend on what has been reported. In all cases, however, the first job is to eliminate any obvious causes. Sadly, many cases fall at this first hurdle. Many incidents, that on first hearing sound promisin,g happen to people who are tired, stressed and open to flights of imagination.

Only if the case survives this initial search for natural explanations is it worth pursuing any further. In the case of recurrent phenomena, such as ghosts, it might be possible to monitor the area to see if you can observe it for yourself. Even if you do 'see' something, it is still important to eliminate any normal explanations first (see Chapter 2, 'Hauntings').

• BEFORE YOU START •

There are one or two cautions to consider before you start to investigate anomalous phenomena. Remember that in your enthusiasm to prove the case, you still need to show consideration to other people, the law and the environment. Some specific points to bear in mind are:

'Many incidents ... happen to people who are tired, stressed and open to flights of imagination.'

- ◇ Always respect any witness' requests for confidentiality. This applies to locations as well as people.
- ◇ Never enter any premises without first getting permission.
- ◇ Only bring in third parties (such as specialists or the media) by prior consent.
- ◇ If a witness refuses to cooperate, always withdraw gracefully.
- ◇ Always maintain a professional, impartial relationship with witnesses.

Remember that you have no special privileges as an investigator, you still have to obey laws and observe social niceties as you would in everyday life.

BACKGROUND RESEARCH

Although many paranormal phenomena are introduced here, there is obviously a great deal more information on them than can be discussed in this book. It is advisable to read other books on specific paranormal subjects along with this one. These will help to give you a good grounding in what sort of events to expect. You should not, however, allow accounts from other books to influence your observations of the case you are investigating. It is a good idea to form your own theories based on experience of cases, rather than solely accepting written reports. Sadly, many books about the paranormal present a definitive view on particular subjects that colour their case accounts.

To remain objective, it is a good idea to join a paranormal society, such as one of those mentioned on page 144, before doing any investigations. Such societies frequently offer training and advice in how to conduct investigations. You can also learn from the experience of other active investigators in such a framework. These societies also offer a place to publish any of your findings. If your case is to make a difference to the world at large it will need to be published somewhere, so it is well worthwhile getting involved with them.

INVESTIGATING

GETTING ON
THE CASE

W HERE DO STRANGE CASES come from? A case originates as a report by someone of an unusual event that has been witnessed. Sometimes, you will come across one through the media, such as in a newspaper. These cases can prove problematic if the people who have reported the event are just out to seek publicity. A far better source of cases is through friends and acquaintances. If you spread the word that you are interested in the paranormal, it is amazing how many strange stories will come your way.

Once you have a case, how do you start investigating it? The vast majority of cases are one-off incidents. Generally your only access to the facts of such an incident is through interviewing witnesses, so this is where you need to start.

'It is important to understand that people are fallible as witnesses.'

• WHAT TO EXPECT FROM WITNESSES •

It is important to understand that people are fallible as witnesses. People, unlike machines, do not react in a predictable way as they interpret what they see. Video recorders, on the other hand, behave in a set way. They simply transfer what is viewed, via a video camera, onto tape. The interpretation of events by people, however, depends on their knowledge, experience and beliefs, and the process happens without the person even being aware of it.

THE INTERPRETATION PROCESS

This process of interpretation starts from the time people experience something. If someone has seen something unusual it is quite normal for them to try to make sense of it. They will search their memory to try and relate it to a similar incident. They will try to fit it in with their beliefs. They will discuss it with friends and relatives or they might consult people they consider to be experts. If you are lucky, they might contact you as an investigator, for your opinion.

The vast majority of people who contact investigators are looking for an explanation of a strange and often disturbing experience. The fact that they are trying to understand the strange event will usually have the effect of altering how it is remembered. Quite often, people who claim to have witnessed incredible sights will, years later, have rationalized them to such an extent that they might even deny what they originally said. People can find strange experiences uncomfortable to live with and will often become sceptical of their own memories.

GETTING REPORTS

To avoid any chang in recall it is important that you should try to interview someone as early as possible after the event. Also, you should try to get information from the witness without adding any interpretation of your own. It might seem obvious to you at the time that a witness has a stone-throwing poltergeist in their house, but do not let that colour your questions. If you focus too much on the stone throwing, you might miss the strange electrical effects that could be accompanying it.

Interviews are, of course, two-way conversations. Without care you may find that in subsequent interviews little embellishments have been added to the witnesses' recollections that tend to confirm your own ideas. The witness has called you in as an expert and will eagerly pick up any theories you expound.

So the most important rules to observe in interviews are:

◇ Try to be neutral.
◇ Always extract the facts from the witness in their own words.
◇ Get them to describe everything that happened without any interruption from you.
◇ Fill in gaps and get extra detail through careful questioning.

• HOW TO INTERVIEW WITNESSES •

Always arrange an interview by appointment and then arrive on time. You should behave in a courteous, professional manner. It is useful if you can go with a colleague, as one of you can be busy framing and asking questions, while the other can pay careful attention to the witness' personality and their surroundings. These last two observations, while subjective, can help to reveal a lot about the circumstances of the case.

INTERVIEW PROCEDURE

At the start of the interview explain to the witness what you are planning to do. Witnesses can become aggrieved if they expect you to get rid of a

'... you should try to interview someone as early as possible after the event.'

nuisance when you are unable or unwilling to do so. If you explain the investigation process at the beginning they will not form unrealistic expectations. You need to stress the investigative nature of your enquiries and explain that you are researching the particular phenomena present to try and understand them.

Stress that you will keep the interview confidential. Also mention that no information will be published (except using pseudonyms for names and addresses) unless they give their permission first. This will help to put the witnesses at their ease.

'Stress that you will keep the interview confidential.'

It is extremely useful to use a tape recorder as detail can be lost if you are constantly writing notes. Of course, you should first ask permission from your witness, but, generally, few refuse. If they are doubtful, emphasize that a tape recording will allow much greater accuracy in getting the facts. It will also allow the conversation to flow more easily without you having to stop to take notes all the time.

Now you need to take down some basic facts such as name, address and any other useful details (see 'Checklist of personal questions', page 20). Then let the witness describe in their own words, without interruption, what they experienced.

Next, try to get more detail about the witness' account. Try to probe for further details, for example, time, place, weather, lighting, other witnesses, colours, smells, and any other things that were going on at the same time to fill in the gaps. The aim is to build up a minute-by-minute account of each incident in full detail so that you get a complete picture of everything that was going on when the incident took place (see 'How to Record an Anomaly', page 20). The questions you ask will, of course, depend on what incident is being reported. You can refer to later chapters to give you more idea of what extra questions you need to ask for different phenomena.

Simple points for interviews

While conducting the interview it is good to remember some simple points:

- Avoid leading questions to get the answer that you want.
- Try not to ask hypothetical questions, which make your own theories obvious, for example, 'could it have been Venus?'.
- Use reflective questions that summarize your own interpretation of what has been said, to see if it is right, for example, 'so it took you ten minutes in total to walk to the office?'.
- Always show interest throughout, and avoid distracting the interviewee with mannerisms, such as playing with your pen.

FINAL QUESTIONS

In the final part of the interview, use questions that probe for possible natural explanations. Some of these will no doubt have occurred to you already. Do not make these too obvious, but try to frame them in a way that will not make it seem as if you are questioning the witness' account, for example, 'and could you see Venus in the sky at the time?' It is important to be subtle about this type of questioning. You may start to leap to premature conclusions and miss important information if you theorize too obvously at this stage. The witness may believe that you are dismissing their observations as being too credulous or ill-informed.

You may need several interviews to get all the facts. Note down if the facts appear to change between interviews. If they change a little this may simply be an indication of the fallibility of memory. Alternatively, it could indicate change under the pressures discussed earlier. But you might also examine the possibility of a hoax (see page 19).

It is important to interview as many witnesses as you can find. Ask your witness if anyone else was around at the time. The best way to approach these new people is by introduction through your main witness, but take care not to give away their identity.

Always treat these secondary witnesses, if they agree to be interviewed, in the same way as the main witness. Obviously, you are looking for corroborative evidence, or otherwise, of the main witness' report. Also, you may find that additional facts emerge that will add to your report.

> ' It is important to interview as many witnesses as you can find. '

POSSIBLE EXPLANATIONS

- **PHYSICAL PHENOMENA**
  Object movement can be due to earth tremors; strange noises to unusual wind direction; odd lights to the aurora; electrical problems to thunder storms.

- **UNUSUAL ANIMAL**
  With a case of an unusual animal you should consult local zoos and private animal collections to see if any inhabitants have gone missing.

- **TRAUMATIC LIFE EVENTS**
  Check for any unusual events in the life of the witness, but ask questions subtly. Clearly unusual, stressful or traumatic life events involving the home or work or health could have an effect on how the witness reacts to incidents.

- **MEDICATION**
  Subtly ask whether the witness was taking medication at the time of the incident as some types can affect perception and even induce hallucinations. This can be included with relevant questions at the beginning of the interview. If the witness becomes suspicious, say it is a standard question that you ask everyone.

- **SLEEP**
  Find out if the event happened on the verge of sleep as people can experience hallucinations at this time. Ask the witness if they felt paralyzed or suffered 'sleep paralysis' (see page 116) during the experience. If all observations were made in this state without witnesses, it would be difficult to substantiate the anomalous occurrence.

• TIME OF THE EVENT •

An important point to note with any anomalous report is *when* the incident occurred. You need to establish if anything unusual was happening at the time of the incident. For instance, a lot of UFO reports these days are filed after laser displays, which are becoming increasingly popular at pop concerts and other special events.

Indeed, with reports of UFOs, the question of what was going on in the sky at the time is crucial. Find out, for example, if there was a meteor shower, a passing bright satellite or a planet on view on the night in question. If such obvious causes of confusion are not eliminated, a UFO report has little credibility. It may seem astonishing to anyone with an interest in astronomy that someone would report Venus as a UFO, but it does happen.

• REVIEWING THE INCIDENT •

By now you can put together a full picture of everything that was witnessed in the event. But is that all there is to it? When a car accident is reported to the police, officers will often go to the crash area to look for skid marks or other traces of what happened. Being involved in an accident is in many ways similar to witnessing the anomalous. Witnesses are often shocked by seeing something out of their ordinary experience. In this state their memory often does not serve them well, so examining the scene can help form a complete picture of what did (and did not) happen.

Suppose, for instance, you were told that a UFO was seen flying across a road in front of the witness' car at hedge height. You might visit the site and find woods on both sides. This probably means that things could not have taken place as described. Perhaps the witness is confused and their memory unclear. Whatever the cause, the discrepancy must be resolved. Possibly take the witness back to the scene to show you where it happened. If, on the other hand, the scene is exactly as was described to you, it lends credibility to the witness' memory.

'It may seem astonishing ... that some- one would report Venus as a UFO, but it does happen.'

VISITING THE SCENE

When you go back to the scene of the incident the first things to do are:

◇ Draw a plan, ideally to scale. You may need a tape measure and compass for this. For a large outdoor site, you may be able to use a large-scale map.

◇ Mark on your plan everything that you come across. Then add in the important points such as the position of witnesses and the apparent track or position of the phenomenon.

◇ Note whether the site is likely to have been seen by pedestrians, other drivers or local people at the time of the incident.

❖ Perhaps place a discreet advert in a local shop to bring forward other witnesses. If there are no such witnesses, you may wonder about the nature of the report. A big cat seen on a busy golf course in the middle of the day, for example, would almost certainly have been seen by several people. If not, ask yourself why.

❖ Take photographs of all the important points in the incident. Put an object of known size in the field of view to act as a scale marker. Shoot the whole scene from different angles as well as taking details of particular points.

❖ For a phenomenon that may have left any marks, such as unusual paw prints, photograph any likely places where these might be, even if you cannot see them at the time. It might be possible to examine the photograph at a later date for clues.

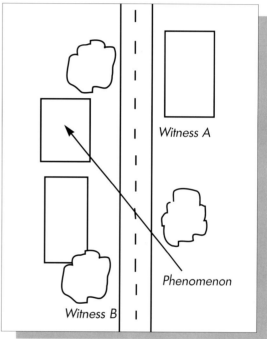

❖ Finally, look at the scene again. Try to imagine what happened by playing out the original incident in your mind's eye. Ideally, do this at the same time of day as the phenomenon reported. Sometimes you will notice things that were not apparent from the original report or your first site examination. You might, for instance, find objects not mentioned in the witness' account that could have a bearing on the case. If the witness is present, it may help to bring to mind further details of the incident.

• A PLAN
Draw a plan of where the incident occured, adding details relating to the phenomenon.

• USING RECONSTRUCTIONS •

Sometimes, reconstructing incidents at the original site can lead to a normal explanation of the incident. Supposing, for instance, a weird groaning noise was reported in a derelict building. On visiting the site you may notice that the wind produces just such a noise when it blows through the ruin from a particular direction.

Such things are likely to be noticed only by making a site visit. Indeed, several visits would be necessary for the type of phenomena just mentioned. Other odd noises, or smells, could be produced by animals or nearby vegetation. Similar unusual effects might be noticed with light where the sun might illuminate only one part of a building for a few minutes at a particular time of year (usually midsummer or midwinter when it is at an extreme of its path in the sky).

If, as a result of your original interviews, you have formed some theories for natural explanations to account for the report, now is the time to try them out. If you think a report of a big cat was actually an ordinary domestic variety seen in such a way that its size was exaggerated, check out your theory.

You could make a full size cardboard cut-out of a domestic cat and put it where the witness saw it. Stand at the same spot as the witness and observe its size. Objects on the skyline can look exaggerated, as a result of an optical illusion.

• BACKGROUND RESEARCH •

You have by now looked at the two most important characteristics of any case – the witness and the site where the incident took place. But there are further things to consider.

Look at the history of the site. If similar occurrences to the one you are investigating have happened there, clearly that is important. Equally, if it has a history of different strange occurrences, that is also interesting. The former may suggest a real objective phenomenon. The latter could mean that some common local factor is causing a whole range of phenomena (or possibly that a place with a 'reputation' leads to suggestion).

'Different phenomena may be interpreted in different ways ...'

Check whether the occurrences are different interpretations of the same natural phenomenon. For instance, abandoned mine workings may give rise to strange noises (caused by wind in the tunnels), which may be reported as ghosts by some people. If the mines cause subsidence, you may hear talk of poltergeists if objects are seen to move without human intervention.

Investigate the cultural context. A reincarnation case would be considered unremarkable in the East, while many in the West would regard it as incredible. This would change the level of evidence that a witness might consider before submitting a report.

Different phenomena may be interpreted in different ways depending on local beliefs. A large animal seen near Loch Ness, for example, would almost inevitably be linked to the Loch Ness monster. Elsewhere it might be interpreted as a different local monster or possibly an escaped zoo animal. So always examine local beliefs, including those of your witnesses. Check for this type of information in local libraries, newspapers and archives. The witnesses themselves could also supply information, as could neighbours.

When talking to neighbours, the local newspaper or police station make sure that you do not compromise the confidentiality of your main witnesses.

Best of all, try and visit a local history society as they can be very informative and can often answer most of your queries.

'Even in good cases the phenomena are usually highly elusive ...'

• WATCH FOR HOAXES •

Regrettably, hoaxes do occur and you should always keep that possibility in the back of your mind. Once, it was said that people would never hoax cases because, by reporting anomalous phenomena, they might appear mentally unstable. But attitudes have changed. Nowadays, quite rightly, there is little stigma attached to making such reports. Indeed, people can become minor celebrities by reporting strange phenomena.

WHAT TO LOOK FOR IN A HOAX

• *The most important test seems to be, based on experience, looking for the 'too good to be true' factor. Any experienced investigator will tell you that good cases are few and far between. Even in good cases the phenomena are usually highly elusive and very rarely recorded on instruments such as video cameras. So, if someone offers you a video of the perfect 'ghost', you should be suspicious.*

Sometimes people will undoubtedly be attracted to the idea of hoaxing for this reason, and they have very little to lose. If they are exposed as hoaxers they can say they did it to expose the gullibility of the media or investigators.

The points to look out for are:

◆ If the evidence is just too good and the case goes too smoothly, think again. Treat the case as a good one but look out for anything suspicious.

◆ Look at the motivation. Are the people looking for fame? People will do some extraordinary things to get media coverage these days. Reporting a ghost is clearly one way of doing it. If your witness seems very keen to get on television or into the newspapers be wary.

Other things to watch for include: changing stories, vagueness and evasiveness during interviews. You could ask witnesses to sign interview statements, if you like. They may be reluctant to do this if they are involved in a deliberate hoax.

• HOW TO RECORD AN ANOMALY •

Every apparently anomalous event reported by the witness should be recorded in as much detail as possible.

Identify every incident where something anomalous apparently occurred. You can work these out from the original interview. Write down what single aspect of the incident made it appear paranormal.

State it in simple descriptive terms without attempting to classify or label it, for example, rather than saying 'Mrs S then saw a 17th-century ghost', put 'Mrs S then saw a figure, apparently in 17th-century costume, move across her living room'. This last description is more precise and it contains no beliefs or interpretations.

Now ask yourself what points about the observation would seem to exclude a natural explanation. In the example above you might find that Mrs S was alone in the house, with locked doors and windows, so it is unlikely to have been a passing stranger.

You then need to ask, if she was alone, is there any evidence of this. Were the doors definitely locked or is she not sure. Another point about the observation that suggests a paranormal explanation is the 17th-century costume. How do you know it is from the 17th-century? Can you narrow it down to any decade within that century? Does the cos-tume make sense, for example, would a particular coat have been worn with that style of breeches and boots described?

See if you can think of any natural explanations for the observation. Does the figure described seem to match characters in a period drama? Check for reflective surfaces and a TV. How convinced are you that this observation is really anomalous?

Checklist of personal questions

The following checklist applies to all investigations, and the aim is to get some information about the witness to try and identify any personal factors that may have impaired perception, to see what the witness wants from the investigator and to find out if the witness has a long history of experiencing strange phenomena. Extra questions needed for specific phenomena will be mentioned in later chapters.

• Ask for name, address, age, occupation (note especially if they do shift work or a repetitive job).

• Talk to them about their health – do they have any deficiencies of hearing, sight or do they suffer from epilepsy or allergies. Also check whether they regularly use prescribed drugs or tranquillizers.

• Find out about religious or spiritual beliefs, interests and hobbies and their attitude to the paranormal. Check whether they were interested in the paranormal before their incident.

• Discreetly ask if there have been any recent stressful experiences, such as a bereavement or a divorce.

• Discover why the witness chose to report the case, and find out if it has been reported to the media.

• Finally, ask if the witness has had any previous paranormal experiences, especially similar ones.

◆ For background information, record such things as: date, time, duration, exact position, weather, state of lighting and temperature.

◆ What about the witness? What were they doing when the incident occurred? Was anything else going on that might have distracted the witness?

◆ Check about the phenomenon itself. What did it do? What was its colour, size, smell, distance, velocity, loudness, speech and feel. Has it been seen before, and if so was it similar? Compare it with common objects to get estimates of magnitude.

◆ Did the phenomenon leave any physical trace or residue which could be analyzed? Is there a video or other recording?

In summary: from each incident you need (a) the characteristics and magnitude of the phenomenon and (b) the degree of proof that it was not a 'normal' observation misinterpreted.

HAUNTINGS

GHOSTS AND POLTERGEISTS

W HAT EXACTLY IS A GHOST? We are all familiar with ghosts from television, films, plays and books. The ghost often appears as a character, taking an active part in its own fate – a conscious spirit that returns to earth with some definite purpose. The ghost of fiction may be forced to haunt the scene of its death as a result of some macabre accident or a terrible wrong committed during life. Fascinating though these fictional portrayals are, they are often as wide of the mark as the child covered in a sheet playing a Hallowe'en game.

• GHOSTLY REALITIES •

The word 'ghost', or 'apparition', actually has a surprisingly wide definition among paranormal researchers. A ghost may be said to be the appearance of a person or animal (or indeed an object, such as a stage-coach) that 'should not be there'. There are many possible reasons why the apparition should not be there, including the obvious: that the person is known to be dead. Another reason could be that a living person is simply known to be geographically elsewhere at the time.

A typical example is the crisis apparition. This is a vision (or indeed some other sign) of a relative or friend at a crisis point in their lives, such as death or a life-threatening situation. Usually the timing and nature of the crisis is unknown to the observer of the apparition. The idea that apparitions are seen when the person is still alive comes as a surprise to many people with traditional notions of ghosts.

Other facts from properly investigated cases will also astonish many journalists and scriptwriters. For example, ghosts are usually described as solid and looking like living people. Indeed, they look so normal that on many occasions the witness only becomes aware of having seen a ghost after it has gone. This is usually because the apparition did

'The word "ghost", or "apparition", actually has a surprisingly wide definition ...'

22

something seemingly 'impossible', such as appear and disappear or walk through a wall. How many ghosts are missed simply because they are never seen to do anything unusual?

UNUSUAL PHENOMENA

Another interesting observation from investigations is that many ghosts appear to perform the same act every time they are seen. For instance, they might walk along a corridor, turn and look left and then walk through a wall. During this performance they show no apparent knowledge of their surroundings (see 'The Cheltenham Ghost', page 35) and rarely seem to see or acknowledge any witnesses. They might even walk along routes that no longer exist, using corridors and doors from a previous building. A ghost might also seem to walk on a level below the current floor. This has been recorded at York, England, in a cellar below the Treasurer's House. The top halves only of Roman soldiers have been observed walking on a previous lower level road. Events such as these, seem to suggest a sort of 'recording' being replayed from time to time.

Ghosts are frequently part of a much wider set of phenomena. A ghost may often be merely one of the things witnessed in a building which is said to be haunted. Indeed, hauntings can take place where no apparitions are seen at all! Additional phenomena might include noises (such as voices, footsteps or raps), cold breezes, moving objects, malfunctioning electrical equipment and unusual smells, each with no known natural cause. Such phenomena would lead a researcher to judge that a building was haunted, whether or not an apparition is involved.

• THE BROWN LADY
This photograph of a ghost on the stairs of Raynham Hall, Norfolk, was taken in 1936.

GHOSTS AND POLTERGEISTS

A haunting may also involve a poltergeist. This phenomenon is named after the German for 'noisy spirit' and is not really a ghost at all. The main characteristic of poltergeist hauntings is that they concentrate on physical activities with a definite emphasis on object movement, noises, changes in heat and light effects. Although they can involve apparitions, they often do not. Another significant difference is that poltergeist cases usually revolve around the presence of a particular person or 'focus'. They also tend to have a finite lifetime (often just weeks or months), whereas other types of ghostly hauntings may rumble on, albeit at a much lower level of activity, for years or even centuries.

The picture most people have of ghosts probably owes more to popular culture than reality. This reinforces the need to investigate such cases without preconceived ideas. If you feel disappointed that the ghosts of fiction do not happen in real life, do not despair. Although ghosts may not correspond to their popular image, that hardly makes them 'normal', and even less, explained. They remain, on existing evidence, a challenge to current scientific thinking. This is why careful, accurate recordings of these extraordinary events are vital to our understanding of them. The challenge facing investigators is to convince scientists that such things really happen and somehow to explain them.

COMPARING HAUNTINGS AND POLTERGEISTS

	HAUNTING	POLTERGEIST
Apparitions seen	Sometimes	Sometimes
Always in same place	Yes	Often follows a person
Duration	Often long-lived	Usually weeks or months
Type of phenomena	Mainly sensory	Mainly physical
Magnitude of phenomena	Usually low level	Often quite intense
Typical phenomena	Footsteps heard, cool breezes felt	Objects moved, lights seen

• TRYING TO SEE A GHOST FOR YOURSELF •

A paranormal researcher should be a neutral observer, not allowing preconceived beliefs to get in the way of observation. For example, if you watched a person in 18th-century costume walk past you in a building that you thought was empty, you might conclude it was a ghost. But how do you definitely know it was not an actor trying to practise their role away from prying eyes? The chances of such a situation may be small, but it cannot be ruled out. But supposing you had locked all entrances to the building and checked all windows were shut, with the only keys safe in your possession. You have now effectively eliminated the possibility of a passing actor dropping in unannounced. This is known as imposing 'controls'. You have eliminated one possible natural cause in your search for an explanation. The more controls you can impose on a situation, the more scientifically acceptable any evidence will become. Even if you have eliminated all such possibilities, your observation might still not be accepted by scientists. Have at least one companion

'The challenge . is to convinc scientists that such things reall happen ...

THE MIAMI POLTERGEIST

In 1967 a classic poltergeist case took place in Miami, in the United States. It was investigated by paranormal researcher William G. Roll who was able to witness incidents himself. The case centred around one particular person who worked in a wholesale warehouse. Objects within the store would fly from their shelves when no one was in the vicinity.

Witnesses observed the objects – novelty souvenirs – flying horizontally off the shelves and then falling vertically to the ground. A magician who examined the case found no evidence of fraud. Roll deliberately placed certain target items for the poltergeist to move. In doing this he could be sure they had not been tampered with in advance of any incident. Also he could be sure, if they were moved, exactly where they had come from. One such object was indeed thrown and could only have reached its destination by flying over or around another untouched item! Object movement happened only within a certain distance of the 'focus'. Events often coincided with times of emotional stress for the 'focus'.

with you. If they report the same figure without any prompting on your part, it will greatly enhance the scientific credibility of the case.

But human beings remain poor recorders of information. To be truly acceptable to science, you need to add another scientific factor in the shape of recording instruments, such as a camera or tape recorder. Most of the paranormal or anomalous phenomena that are examined in this book tend to occur unpredictably. Luckily ghosts and poltergeists involve relatively frequent phenomena at a particular place. So if we can set up instruments and position observers in controlled conditions in such places, we have a chance to make scientifically credible observations of the paranormal. Researchers call such stake-outs 'vigils'.

· PREPARING A VIGIL ·

A vigil involves a lot of work and is not something to be embarked upon half-heartedly. Preparation is paramount.

◇ INTERVIEW WITNESSES

Do this before the vigil so that researcher's own experiences do not colour witness responses (see page 14).

◇ GET PERMISSION TO HOLD A VIGIL FROM THE BUILDING OWNERS

This should be in writing. Take the permission with you to the vigil, as such written permission can even help on the night. There have been instances where the police have noticed vigils and called in to see what was going on! Also, offer to pay for any power or heating that you use on the vigil.

◇ SELECT PEOPLE TO GO ON THE VIGIL CAREFULLY

Ideally, you need people without strong beliefs who share your neutral approach. It is useful to have one or two specialists. These could be expert photographers, sound recordists and others with relevant technical abilities, who would be able to bring their own specialist equipment (see 'Instruments to Use on a Vigil' page 27). All vigil participants must agree to abide by any rules and instructions issued by the vigil organizer during the night.

◇ DO NOT TELL PEOPLE WHAT TO EXPECT

Nobody taking part in the vigil should be told anything about the haunting before the vigil. If they then witness something on the night that agrees with previous reports, it obviously greatly strengthens the case.

◇ CHECK OUT THE VENUE IN ADVANCE

Research the venue beforehand, not just the paranormal history of the building but also its layout. Much of this information will have been derived from the site investigation. You need to know practical information such as the location of power points for equipment. You can seek out suitable places to station observers and equipment to capture the phenomena. One problem with deploying people and equipment at places where phenomena have been seen is that it may give the game away to people on the vigil. Set up additional stations where nothing has been reported in order to safeguard against this.

' ... you need people without strong beliefs who share your neutral approach. '

◇ RECORD POSSIBLE 'NATURAL EXPLANATIONS' IN ADVANCE

On your trip to check out the venue, look for any natural phenomena, such as creaking floorboards, that are likely to be confused for paranormal ones. A common source of odd noises is central heating systems cooling at night. Look out for sources of stray reflections too. These can then be taken into account when examining reports at the end of the vigil.

◇ PREPARE VIGIL EQUIPMENT

Equipment on a vigil serves two purposes. One is that it eliminates natural causes, for example, a video camera would see anyone interfering with an object that is supposed to move by itself. The other is to actually record phenomena. There are very few authentic recordings of apparently paranormal phenomena (see 'A Vigil at Dover Castle', page 30). Those that exist have more scientific credibility than hundreds of witness reports.

INSTRUMENTS TO USE ON A VIGIL		
Instrument	Usage	Notes
ANEMOMETER	Measures wind speed	
AUDIO TAPE RECORDER	For audio notes in the dark and recording such things as raps or footsteps	
BAROMETER	Records air pressure	
HYGROMETER	Measures atmospheric humidity	
MAGNETOMETERS	Records changes in local magnetic field	
STILL CAMERA	Recording phenomena	Digital are especially useful (can go directly onto a computer)
THERMOMETERS	To look for 'cold' spots and paranormal breezes	Try to get electronic versions
VIDEO CAMERA	Recording phenomena and as a control	Modern types are often usable in low light

◇ THE VARIETY OF EQUIPMENT

Some equipment, such as the Passive Infrared (PIR) detector acts to control natural causes. It detects movement that occurs in front of it and so should be placed in an empty room. Other equipment is for recording phenomena (see above). Other instruments can be used to record things that people cannot sense, for example, radiation by Geiger counters or magnetism using a magnetometer. A specialist would need to analyze these types of readings.

◇ DO A PRACTICE RUN WITH EQUIPMENT BEFORE A VIGIL

Always have a practice run with any new instrument before going out on a vigil, to see how reliable and sensitive it is. Also find out what effect everyday objects have on it, and verify how long batteries last or if anything needs adjusting over long periods. Familiarize yourself with equipment such as videos or magnetometers. If something is difficult to operate, produce simple instructions for others to use it. Check the calibration of instruments, particularly Geiger tubes, if they have not been used for a while.

◇ PLAN EXACTLY WHERE TO PUT INSTRUMENTS

Position instruments where they cannot move. Try to deploy

'A single investigator should never be left on his or her own ...'

instruments close to each other if possible. Clearly, instruments should be placed where they are most likely to 'observe' phenomena, but not so that it becomes obvious to everyone where phenomena are likely to occur. Also have duplicate instruments as a backup in case any machine goes wrong. If possible, try to get instruments that measure the same quantity but rely on different detection mechanisms, for example video cameras with tubes and charge-coupled devices.

◇ SYNCHRONIZE ALL YOUR INSTRUMENTS

This is hard to do in all vigils. If each instrument has its own recording mechanism (possibly human, as in reading a thermometer) you must synchronize them all. Everyone needs to agree the start time, so that you will know whether any unusual reading corresponds with an observed incident or not.

◇ TRY TO AUTOMATE INSTRUMENT READING

Ideally, do automated recording direct to a personal computer (PC) as the amount of data produced is enormous and it can be computer-analyzed at leisure afterwards. It is possible to buy electronic multi-channel boxes that take feeds from various instruments and push them into the serial or parallel connection of a PC. These boxes typically come with software that samples many times per second. Set the clock on the PC at the start, and make sure leads are reasonably short as longer ones can suffer from electrical interference.

ON THE NIGHT

Vigils generally take place at night. This is not because ghosts are more frequently seen at night, but because it is easier to have the building to yourselves then. Also, things are quieter at night, making it easier to pick up faint phenomena. It is not necessary to have all the lights out, but low light conditions may help to create a conducive mood.

The basic principle of conducting a vigil is to split the investigators up into teams of two or more. Each team is then stationed at a particular location to look for phenomena and operate any instruments set up there. You should draw up a rota (see page 29) which moves teams from location to location at regular intervals. It is a good idea to have a short break between each session (or 'watch') for rest.

Everyone taking part in the vigil should be equipped with a notebook, pen, torch and a watch as a basic minimum so that they can log anything they hear, see or feel during the night. Warm clothing may be necessary

'Ghostly footsteps ar a commor feature of hauntings ..

Sample Team Rota

	10–11.30pm	12–1.30am	2–3am	3.30–5am
Door 1	Team A	D	C	B
Stairs	Team B	A	D	C
Hall	Team C	B	A	D
Floor 2	Team D	C	B	A

in many situations. Food and drink should be brought as this helps people to stay awake – but be careful not to bring aromatic or strongly flavoured foods onto a site where anomalous smells have been reported. A walkie-talkie (Citizen's Band radio) for each team could also be useful in case any dramatic incident needs extra people.

Investigators should be asked to remain at a given location for up to one or two hours, after which they should move somewhere else for the next period, to prevent boredom setting in. It is probably a good idea to reserve half an hour during the night for a feedback session when tactics can be reviewed in the light of events.

A single investigator should never be left on his or her own, as there is then no way of proving that they are not responsible for anything that may occur. There is also the possibility that a novice investigator left alone could be 'spooked' by something he or she misidentifies. Bear this is mind during toilet and refreshment breaks, when the team's guard may be down.

If remote monitoring is employed, two investigators should watch the equipment at all times. If a video camera is used, this should be linked to a TV monitor so that anything unusual can be seen and investigated immediately. Regular readings of thermometers need to be taken, as sudden changes of temperature are often reported in cases of a haunting.

Ghostly footsteps are a common feature of hauntings and it can be difficult to be sure that they are not produced by an investigator. You need to address this problem, for example by prohibiting all movement in a corridor where footsteps are said to be heard. The flushing of toilets is a surprisingly common feature: unless it is clearly understood that investigators use the toilet only at changeover times (except in an emergency, in which case it should be noted in the log), any noises from

• VIGIL SET-UP
A ghost is said to walk from door 3 towards door 2. The video camera is in the most likely location to record the ghost. Team A can monitor doors 1 and 2. Team B controls door 3 and corridors 1 and 2.

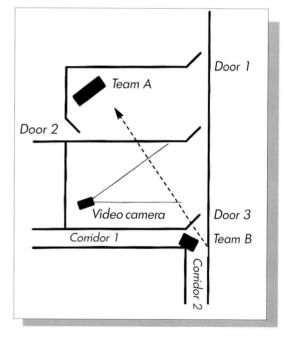

A VIGIL AT DOVER CASTLE, ENGLAND

• DOVER CASTLE
The oldest part
of the castle
dates back to
the 1180s.

Tour guides and local traditions often claim that castles are haunted. Somewhat unusually, Dover's imposing castle, built in the 1180s during the reign of Henry II had no recorded history of hauntings before Robin Laurence started his investigation.

Laurence, a paranormal researcher, became interested in the castle after he heard that staff there had undergone some strange experiences. Robin not only unearthed reports of noises and ghosts in strange dress, but also produced some extraordinary video evidence. Here is an extract from his report, detailing experiences reported by the castle staff:

◇ 'A male figure dressed in early 17th-century costume (Cavalier style, 1610–1630) was seen by a female member of staff in 1990, at around 8.30 a.m., while she was cleaning.

◇ 'Another witness described how a soldier (identified as a 17th-century pikeman) wearing a 'morion' helmet and carrying a pike, walked into the guardroom through one wall and out again through another.

◇ 'During the summer of 1991, an American tourist and his wife commented to a member of the castle staff on the 'very realistic sounds' (screams and moans) which they heard while touring the passageways. The two visitors were the very last to leave the tunnels and thought they had been listening to an audio recording of sound effects. They were the only people in the tunnels at the time.

◇ 'The most commonly reported phenomenon is the sound of heavy wooden doors being slammed shut.'

obin arranged a vigil which took place
n 12 October 1991. The 16 investigators
ere divided into eight teams of two. The
ideo they made must be one of the few
ecordings of poltergeist activity actually
n progress. The logbook entries below

summarize what happened. Research has
not yet established any specific historical
reason for the haunting. The events that
gave rise to it are, as in most such cases,
probably quite mundane and unlikely to
be recorded in history.

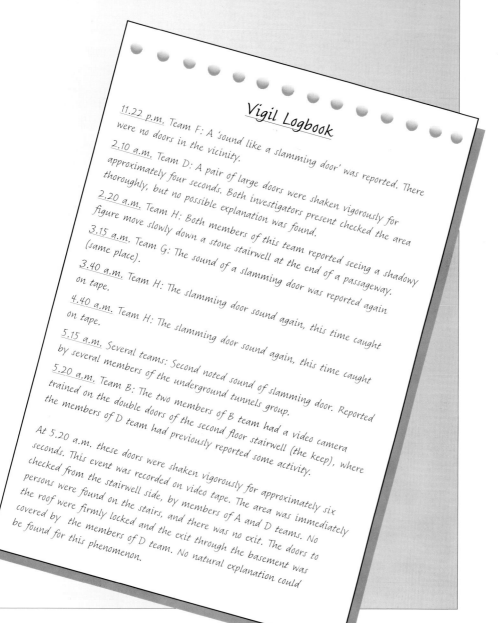

Vigil Logbook

<u>11.22 p.m.</u> Team F: A 'sound like a slamming door' was reported. There were no doors in the vicinity.

<u>2.10 a.m.</u> Team D: A pair of large doors were shaken vigorously for approximately four seconds. Both investigators present checked the area thoroughly, but no possible explanation was found.

<u>2.20 a.m.</u> Team H: Both members of this team reported seeing a shadowy figure move slowly down a stone stairwell at the end of a passageway.

<u>3.15 a.m.</u> Team G: The sound of a slamming door was reported again (same place).

<u>3.40 a.m.</u> Team H: The slamming door sound again, this time caught on tape.

<u>4.40 a.m.</u> Team H: The slamming door sound again, this time caught on tape.

<u>5.15 a.m.</u> Several teams: Second noted sound of slamming door. Reported by several members of the underground tunnels group.

<u>5.20 a.m.</u> Team B: The two members of B team had a video camera trained on the double doors of the second floor stairwell (the keep), where the members of D team had previously reported some activity.

At 5.20 a.m. these doors were shaken vigorously for approximately six seconds. This event was recorded on video tape. The area was immediately checked from the stairwell side, by members of A and D teams. No persons were found on the stairs, and there was no exit. The doors to the roof were firmly locked and the exit through the basement was covered by the members of D team. No natural explanation could be found for this phenomenon.

the toilet will automatically be discounted. The problem of distinguishing anomalous noises from those of a normal origin is a major one, and the organizer needs to plan the vigil with this in mind. The whole point of the exercise can be lost if it cannot be proved that a noise was of paranormal origin.

The final step should be a debriefing session at which the participants can discuss the night's events (or lack of them!). This is often the time when, through comparing notes, it is first realized that something strange has occurred. Ideally this session should be held as soon as everyone has benefited from a good night's sleep, but the organizer should have a brief word at the end of the vigil with anyone who will be unable to attend a later session. Such sessions can be very important in making an assessment of any phenomena that may have occurred, and in deciding what further action needs to be taken. The organizer should also collect all the logs before participants depart.

Debriefing sessions have revealed phenomena that were not even noticed during the actual vigil. There have been numerous occasions when people have reported hearing footsteps and assumed it was another member of the vigil. In the Dover Castle case (see page 30) a shadowy figure was noted on some stairs. At the time, the observers simply assumed that it was a fellow researcher. One wonders what went through their minds when it was later revealed that no one had moved during that watch!

'... it has been noted that close monitoring of phenomena can actually suppress them ...'

• GETTING RID OF GHOSTS •

Paranormal researchers are frequently asked to 'get rid' of the particular phenomena they have come to investigate. This is perfectly understandable as the haunting may be disruptive or frightening to those effected. Naturally, the researcher may not be quite so keen to get rid of the ghost! It is useful to point out to witnesses that we do not yet fully understand these types of paranormal phenomena and need to study them before we can have any hope of getting rid of them. You could try to engage their interest in these fascinating and (almost always) harmless phenomena.

If witnesses are getting very stressed by the phenomena then researchers should try to help diffuse the tension. There are various techniques that you can use:

◇ LISTEN SYMPATHETICALLY
   Point out that other people have had similar experiences. This knowledge can greatly reduce stress. The fact that many, perfectly

THE CASE OF THE VOODOO BIRD

In the late spring of 1996, London-based investigator Phil Walton received a telephone call from a woman whom we will call 'Vicky'. Clearly in some distress, she recounted a tale of a ghost bird that followed its victims about above their heads. The 'bird' had been annoying her for nearly three years, usually in the spring and often in the evening, emitting a loud screeching sound. Phil's initial theory was that birds were nesting in the loft or under the eaves.

They set a date for an initial meeting at Vicky's home. Phil was accompanied by fellow investigator Chris Walton. A site examination revealed a distinct lack of eaves or cavities for any birds to nest in. The walls, floor and roof were all thick concrete.

The investigators then listened to the intriguing tale of how Vicky believed the 'bird' had come to haunt her. She told them that a relative had threatened her with a curse – although the exact form of the curse was not specified.

Vicky said that although she was now a Christian and worshipped at a local church, she had a Jamaican and voodoo background. To get behind her thought processes, Chris researched as much as he could on voodoo.

As usual in cases where the witness is the main observer, the investigators asked Vicky to keep a diary of events recording such things as the weather, time, date and how she felt at the time of each incident.

Then Phil received a frantic call from Vicky. She was at home with a relative and the 'bird' was there. They were praying to stop it but it was following them wherever they went. The conversation was interrupted several times by the 'bird's' cry. Phil called Chris and amassed all the equipment he could to capture the sound. To guard against the risk of equipment failure, Phil asked colleagues to switch on their answering machines, so that he could telephone the sound through.

Within five minutes of their arrival, the screech was heard and Phil's years of fiddling with electronic equipment were put to good use. He recognized the sound as that of a piezoelectric sounder, used in fire alarms. This one sounded as if it was malfunctioning. He asked Vicky if she had a fire alarm. With a surprised look she said 'yes'. Then it was Phil's turn to be surprised: the battery clip was hanging out of the case with nothing attached!

Almost immediately there was another squawk. Because of its high pitch and the concrete construction of the building, locating the sound was difficult. It did indeed appear to come from just above head level wherever you were in the building. Eventually they narrowed the source down to a piece of wall above a doorway. After a bit of tapping and the removal of a small patch of wallpaper they finally found the 'bird'. It was a fire alarm that had been wallpapered over. Phil unscrewed it and pushed its test button. It answered with the by now familiar squawk. The voodoo 'bird' has never bothered Vicky since.

Case Log Book

April 1996: Site investigation reveals no obvious causes for the disturbance... Witness suspects that Voodoism is the cause...

May–July 1996: Witness is becoming increasingly frightened. Manifestations of the 'bird' continue at regular intervals.

sane, people have witnessed exactly the same kind of phenomena should be reassuring.

◆ GET WITNESSES TO KEEP A DIARY OF INCIDENTS
Encourage witnesses to take an active, scientific interest in the phenomena. Get them to keep a log book of the phenomena and try to record it on audio or video tape. When people's interest is engaged this usually reduces the stress of the situation. Also, rather oddly, it has been noted that close monitoring of phenomena can actually suppress them. Certainly phenomena often seem to be inhibited by the presence of investigators. No one knows what causes this effect, but it could partially explain why it is so difficult to obtain recordings of paranormal activity.

◆ POINT OUT THAT MANY 'OUTBREAKS' VANISH OF THEIR OWN ACCORD
Poltergeist cases last only for a limited period. The same cannot be said about other hauntings, but these tend not to be as dramatic or frightening.

◆ SUGGEST THE WITNESS CONSULTS A MEDICAL PRACTITIONER
If witnesses continue to have a problem, you could gently suggest that they might want to talk to a medical practitioner about stress management. Do not bring in third party experts such as psychologists or hypnotherapists yourself.

◆ RESIST REQUESTS FOR EXORCISM
It is not the job of the neutral paranormal researcher to get involved in such things as exorcisms. Exorcisms are related to particular belief systems, which the witness may or may not share. Contrary to popular opinion they often do not work and have been reported to aggravate the stress levels in vulnerable people and intensify any anomalous activity that surrounds them. Such an approach could be viewed as unethical and irresponsible.

'Poltergeist cases last only for a limited period.'

· USING MEDIUMS IN INVESTIGATIONS ·

A medium is a person who can apparently gain information or impressions from spiritual sources, rather than the conventional human senses (see also Chapter 10, 'Life After death'). People claiming mediumship have been studied as paranormal phenomena in their own right for some time. There is, as yet, no scientific consensus about the validity of their abilities. Some people seem to be able to consistently

THE CHELTENHAM GHOST

Between 1882 and 1889 reports were received of a spectacular haunting in a house in Cheltenham, England. It was particularly important because it displayed so many characteristics of the 'classic' haunting while being very well observed by a number of credible witnesses.

The ghost, described as a 'tall lady, dressed in black of a soft woollen material', was often seen in the drawing room, usually standing beside a sofa. She always hid part of her face with a handkerchief. After remaining there for some time, she would move to the door, go into the hall and disappear. Any attempts to communicate with her were ignored. She was visible only to certain people, others in the same room could see nothing. Although she was seen to walk through cords that could be moved with the slightest touch, they were left unmoved. Attempts to touch the apparition made it disappear. The ghost was normally accompanied by the sounds of bumps, soft footsteps and door handles being turned.

To the people who saw her, she was solid enough to be mistaken for a real person. A cold breeze was reported among the phenomena associated with her appearance. Interestingly, the ghost never appeared when people deliberately lay in wait for it.

gain information which would not normally be available to them. By introducing a medium into a case you could be adding another 'unknown factor' into a situation already full of uncontrollable variables.

Apparently mediumistic material can also be obtained through cryptomnesia, where someone remembers something while not consciously realizing they ever knew it. They could, for instance, know obscure historical detail without remembering that they read it in a book years ago. However, there are good cases where information has apparently been obtained in extraordinary circumstances, such as when working with the police, mediums have located objects or people involved in crimes with very little information.

In normal circumstances there is no obvious reason to introduce mediums to a case. If you do introduce them, try to bring them in at a late stage, once all the conventional methods of investigation have been exhausted. Always try to assess them first, ask them to volunteer information that you can check out personally for its reliability. Keep any information from them in separate written reports from the conventional evidence.

STRANGE OBJECTS
IN THE SKY

THE TERM 'UFO' SIMPLY STANDS for unidentified flying object. In the vast majority of cases that are reported they are just that, objects that have proved difficult to identify in the sky, or ones that have been seen hovering above the ground. So, if that is all there is to it, why has there been so much film interest, TV coverage, books and societies springing up on the subject over the last few decades?

The reason is far more complicated than just a sighting made on a starry night. It stems from the fact that the term 'UFO' has become clouded with the issues of life on other planets, alien abductions and flying saucers, not to mention government cover-ups and possible involvement of security services.

'The moon and planets are often reported as UFOs ...'

• INVESTIGATING UFOs •

If a UFO report comes your way for investigation you will want to interview the witness and examine the site where the incident happened (see Chapter 1, 'Investigating'). The course of the investigation will be largely dictated by exactly what was reported. So, if you think the object was astronomical, for example, you may want to check the positions of the planets or satellites at the time the incident occurred.

If you think the incident may have involved a plane then you could talk to the aviation or defence authorities to see if there were any aircraft in the area at the appropriate time. Bear in mind that most people are surprisingly unfamiliar with what there is to be seen naturally in the skies and most reports will turn out to have rational explanations. If you are not too familiar with the skies yourself, you would be advised to do a skywatch. This simply consists of staying up all night and watching for anything unusual to happen. On a clear night, away from bright lights, you should definitely see such things as meteors and bright planets and

36

will probably also notice satellites. It also helps to have an astronomy expert on hand. See page 39 for some other natural explanations.

◇ ASTRONOMICAL OBJECTS

About three-quarters of all UFO sightings involve no more than the description of a pinpoint or smudge of light. The moon and planets are often reported as UFOs, usually because the observer sees them in an unfamiliar setting or viewing conditions are poor. The glow from a full moon as it sets can often spark a report. Planets are mostly brighter than stars and also trigger reports. If the planet or moon is then filmed without a tripod, the image is often of a light streaking across the sky, while in reality it is just the motion of a shaky hand. On more than one occasion a witness has described just such an observation. On being told that Jupiter or Venus is particularly bright and visible in the night sky at that moment, the observer will often realize that their UFO was indeed in the same place as the planet, so the UFO becomes an IFO – identified flying object.

◇ MOVING CELESTIAL OBJECTS

Although planets move against a background of stars, their movement is too slow to be noticed in the course of an evening. Comets – large balls of ice, rock and stellar debris – are also slow, but their movement against the stars is visible with binoculars or the naked eye. As they come close to the sun, a large tail will stretch out across the sky.

By contrast, meteors move much faster across the sky. A meteor is a small piece of space debris, about the size of a grain of sand, that leaves a bright trail in the sky as it enters the Earth's atmosphere and burns up. Some are the remains of a comet tail, and it is this collection of comet debris that produces the yearly meteor shower called the Perseids (which reaches a maximum on 12 August) giving a display of up to 60 an hour.

• COMET
Stellar debris is responsible for a number of UFO sightings.

37

'Some man-made satellites can be seen from the Earth's surface.'

Much rarer are meteorites. These are larger bits of rock, usually about the size of a briefcase, that make it through the Earth's atmosphere and hit the Earth. They are much brighter, but just as fast, and are visible for only a few seconds. Some of these larger bits of rock may explode as they come into the atmosphere and this produces a bright flash called a bolide, with many smaller pieces splitting off and continuing their journey to the Earth. Sometimes the angle of entry into the atmosphere is so shallow that the rock skims on the outer atmosphere and bounces back out into space. After many years as an amateur astronomer and an avid sky watcher, the author was rewarded recently with a bolide that did just that. It streaked across the late afternoon sky with a brilliance that would have outshone a full moon.

◇ ATMOSPHERIC LIGHT SHOWS

The aurora borealis and aurora australis are both light shows caused by the sun's solar wind (a stream of charged particles) being captured by the Earth's magnetic field. The ghostly lights are prominent near the Earth's poles, changing with the density and speed of the solar wind. Sometimes they can be seen at lower latitudes. The 'Northern Lights' have been seen as far south as London, where, sadly, streetlights tend to swamp the effect.

◇ MAN-MADE OBJECTS

Some man-made satellites can be seen from the Earth's surface. They do not produce any light of their own (except in the case of Mir and the international space station) but reflect the sun's. Because of this, they are usually only visible a few hours after sunset and a few hours before sunrise, when the observer is in the shadow of the Earth and the satellite is high enough still to be illuminated. Most satellites look like a moving star slowly crossing the sky. They may appear or disappear suddenly anywhere in the sky as they leave or enter the Earth's shadow.

• WEATHER BALLOON
Even man-made objects can be mistaken for UFOs.

DAY TIME NATURAL CAUSES OF UFOS

PHENOMENON	APPEARANCE
Lenticular clouds	Saucer-shaped clouds
Hot-air balloons	Can appear as bright stationary objects if they catch the sun. They are especially dramatic at twilight
Planes	Can appear as bright moving objects if they catch the sun; especially dramatic at twilight
Birds	High flying large birds can appear as dark dots

NIGHT TIME NATURAL CAUSES OF UFOS

PHENOMENON	APPEARANCE
Planets	Some planets appear as very bright stars, particularly Venus which is often seen in twilight above where the sun has just set or is about to rise
Moon	Causes a glow on the horizon when setting
Satellite	Looks like a slowly moving star
Meteor/Bolide	A fast moving 'star' with a tail
Aurora	Rapidly moving patches of coloured lights (often like luminous curtains) usually only seen at high latitudes
Light shows	Light shows (especially with lasers) show up as beams of light and illuminated clouds
Planes	Close formation of moving lights, often flashing; a sound may also come from another part of the sky
Earthlights/ Marsh lights/ Ball lightning	Bright balls of light floating (usually) low above the ground
Fireflies	Small lights seen floating near the ground that often flash

Mir, the large Russian space station, and the new international space station are in a different league. You can observe the equivalent of a sunset as Mir enters the shadow of the Earth. It reflects enough light that has passed through a sideways section of the atmosphere to turn red just like the sun or moon. The new space station will be so large and in such an orbit that it will be one of the brightest objects in the night sky!

Laser shows and circus arc lights are responsible for many reports of UFOs. The ability of these lights to bounce off high cloud, focus in and out, and to be seen from many miles away make them strange sights to people who are not used to the night sky.

High-flying planes, airships, weather balloons, helicopters and hot-air balloons can also be difficult to recognize. At night you may only see the flare of an aircraft's engines as it turns or the very bright lights it uses to warn others of its presence. Landing lights can be seen from great distances and often fool the observer into thinking they are going one way when in reality they are turning or going in the other direction. This can mislead the observer into thinking that the object is standing still or is moving off at great speed.

Often the observer says that it could not be a plane, as they did not hear it. Weather conditions can cause this effect. If the observer is in cold air and there is a warm front between him and a plane, then the sound may not penetrate but bounce off the front. The observer will see but not hear the aircraft, or hear a sound from a different part of the sky (an effect similar to a mirage but involving sound rather than light). Even in normal weather conditions the sound of an aircraft will always come from a different part of the sky from where it is visible. This is simply because light travels much faster than sound.

◇ WEATHER EFFECTS

Some of the best UFO photographs are of lenticular clouds. They can form singly or in clusters, are slow moving, stable and often disc-shaped. Indeed, they often clearly resemble the classic 'flying saucer' shape beloved of movie makers, making them a good subject for photography.

• LENTICULAR
CLOUD
These bizarrely shaped clouds resemble the 'flying saucers' of popular fiction.

Until recently ball lightning was thought to be folklore, but in the last decade many credible witnesses have come forward. Ball lightning was assumed to be impossible but, as this book was being written a scientist in Spain has put forward a plausible explanation of the physics behind the phenomenon. It is thought that ball lightning is formed in thunderclouds, as there is a strong correlation with lightning storms and ball lightning. Witnesses report seeing a sphere about the size of a football, which can move towards or away from the observer. It lasts for up to a minute and then dissipates. If it touches another object it can leave scorch marks as it disintegrates.

Even if a person is familiar with their surroundings and the night sky, they would probably find it hard to rationalize a ball of light seen hovering over the ground seeming to interact with the landscape, and which then suddenly disappears.

◇ GEOLOGICAL LIGHTS

Marshes and similar boggy areas can give rise to a phenomenon known as 'will-o'-the-wisp' or *ignis fatuus*. The lights are greenish in colour and move with a fluid motion over surrounding surfaces.

40

The phenomenon is thought to be caused by the spontaneous ignition of marsh gases reacting with oxygen in the air when they reach the surface of the water.

Researcher Paul Devereux has put forward a geological theory to explain certain UFO sightings. In his 'earth lights' theory, balls of light are produced, mainly along geological fault lines, by the piezoelectric effect. This is when quartz crystals are compressed so that they produce an electric charge which can discharge (for example, as a spark) if the voltage is big enough. Devereux theorizes that in seismically active areas with quartz rocks the huge forces involved may trigger electric discharges in the form of balls of light that float freely in the air. Clearly, as in the case of will-o'-the-wisp, such lights could easily be mistaken for UFOs.

FIREFLIES

• *Fireflies, the small luminous flying insects that can be seen in rural areas and often stun city-dwellers by the strength of the light they are capable of producing, are often mistaken for alien invaders. They are capable, at close quarters, of strongly illuminating the surrounding vegetation and they are not the only creatures to possess this trick.*

◇ BEYOND NORMAL EXPLANATIONS

'But it wasn't any of the above, I'm sure it was a UFO', is the cry often heard from some people when given a rational explanation of something they have seen. Looking closely at this statement is getting to the heart of the whole UFO/alien problem. What people really want is a definitive explanation of what they saw. So often the reason that they could not identify it as one of the above is because at the time of seeing the object, their senses failed due to the speed of the event or the less-than-perfect observing conditions.

We have an inbuilt need to identify objects as familiar and if they don't fit the stored images that we have in our brains, we try to make them fit by jumping to fanciful explanations. Finally, we are overwhelmed with enough information to drop our wrong identification. But if we don't have the luxury of a closer look we are left with the original conclusion, even if it is wrong.

· HOW THE TERM 'UFOS' CAME ABOUT ·

The ongoing interest in alien life on other planets has been fostered by many TV programmes and films, but how exactly did UFOs become so popular as a concept? To find out more we need to look at the history of UFO phenomenon.

' ... most UFO craft are described as a disc, cigar or triangle-shaped ...'

The afternoon of Tuesday 24 June 1947 marks the start of the UFO meta-morphosis. There had already been one previous use of the term 'flying saucer' on 25 January 1878 by a Texan farmer, John Martin, but this did not attract much interest. It took Kenneth Arnold, a private pilot searching for a crashed cargo plane, to attract the public's interest, and herein lies the twist, for he was misquoted and what he did not say caught on!

As he looked out of his small private plane searching for a crashed C46 Marine Corps transport plane, his attention was caught by a flash of light in his cockpit, then another on the wing of his plane. The only other aircraft in the sky was a DC4. In the distance he made out nine lights moving erratically, coming from the vicinity of Mount Baker in the Cascade Range, Washington State, USA. He described the objects as being like discs with a bit taken out, similar to a boomerang.

The term 'flying saucer' comes from the description of how they flew, like the tail of a Chinese kite or 'like a saucer would if you skipped it across water'. Arnold thereby started an all-encompassing interest. But the witnesses that followed did not see what he saw, they saw what the press reported he saw. In fact, most UFO craft are described as disc-, cigar- or triangle-shaped object that move very fast in straight lines not, as Arnold observed, in a wavy pattern.

So what did Arnold actually see? Many have speculated as to the origin of the fast moving lights. Arnold himself did not think that they were craft from another world, but the media exploited the idea in the minds of the public.

My speculation is that Arnold observed reflections from another object, perhaps a lorry or car, moving along the roads below, or from the DC4. My reasoning comes from my days working in plant nurseries. On rare occasions when looking down on a series of glasshouses from a hill above, you could observe the shaky movement of the sun bouncing from the glass onto clouds. If the reflective object was moving, the description could be of a series of lights moving at speed and waving up and down. The initial flash could have been a direct beam of light from the object into the cockpit (he was turning through 180 degrees at the time and so the cockpit would have been opened up to a reflection from below). It's a simpler and more likely explanation than a fleet of interstellar spacecraft unobserved by anyone else or radar, but the honest answer is that we just don't know. There was insufficient information then and there is certainly no more to add now.

With the sudden wave of UFO sightings all across America and with 'craft' reportedly filling up the night sky, it was hardly surprising that one would eventually crash (see 'The Crash - Roswell', right). And sure enough, with the media interest in flying saucers at a peak and every

THE CRASH – ROSWELL

On 2 July 1947, 50 kilometres (31 miles) from Corona in a desolate area of New Mexico, USA, an explosion was heard by a farmer during a thunderstorm. The next day he found the silvery remains of 'something' which was not easy to identify.

Rancher William 'Mac' Brazel discovered what seemed to be half a mile of thin light metal and balsa wood. Larger pieces resembled aluminium foil. On 6 July he showed some of the debris to the county sheriff, George Wilcox, who reported the find to intelligence officer Major Jesse Marcel at the nearby Roswell Army Air Field base.

After Marcel and a Counter Intelligence Corps agent had inspected the site, the army was called in. On 8 July the area was sealed off and the remains were collected and loaded into a Buick and driven to Roswell. From there the load went to Fort Worth, Texas and on to Patterson Field (Wright Field in 1947), Dayton, Ohio.

Much of the material was described as silver and it was reported that, if you screwed it up, it opened back to its original shape. These are all properties of aluminized plastics that existed then, although at the time these were new, still secret and were used for balloons.

However, at this time there was no mention of the 'alien bodies' found at Roswell that later starred in the *Autopsy* film and at the time the incident only merited a few local newspaper articles.

One reason why Roswell later gained such notoriety was that it was initially reported as a 'flying saucer' by the military themselves. This statement was then hastily withdrawn. This single action (apparently to conceal a then secret project) could be the key to subsequent events leading to other tales of cover-ups.

What is agreed is that something crashed that day. What was shown at the time, and what was officially admitted, was that a weather balloon came down in a storm on the night of 2 July 1947. No bodies, no spacecraft. The instruments it carried were most likely monitoring equipment flown high to look for flashes over the horizon, the sign of an emerging nuclear nation, the Soviet Union.

However, in 1994 after an investigation by US Congressman Steven Schiff, it was revealed that the debris was not from a weather balloon, but from a top-secret experiment that had to be protected at all costs. But the question still remains why this was not revealed in the intervening years when the project was long dead.

'... tales are still being told of aliens being dragged screaming from the spacecraft ' ...

state, bar two, reporting at least one, the inevitable happened. That it happened was not a surprise, but that it was less than a month after Arnold's sighting is surprising.

It was not until the 1960s and early 1970s that the legends of Roswell started to gain extra 'facts'. Fifty years on and tales are still being told of aliens being dragged screaming from the spacecraft and being shot as they cried out. Artists' impressions of intergalactic craft at Roswell appeared together with tales of US government holding areas full of bodies and craft. And yet at the recent reunion of the 509 Bomb Group – the Corps that took away the crash debris – in 1996, the retired men all denied that there was ever a 'crashed saucer'. They stated that the debris that was removed would have filled no more than a wheelbarrow.

· ALIEN CONTACT ·

It was not long after the Roswell incident that UFOs and alien sightings became familiar news stories. Tales of contact with aliens soon became popular and stories of abduction and experimentation continue. This triggered new research techniques, such as hypnotic regression, in order to try and understand the shared experiences of so many people.

ALIEN MESSAGES

It needs to be considered why aliens would use contactees such as George Adamski (see 'George Adamski', right) to pass on information that we already know. No contactee told us of aliens' warning about global warming or the ozone hole before we discovered these things, when it would have been useful.

In many accounts the aliens seem to have already been through the problems we face, so why not tell us before we suffer them? Could it be that the warnings are coming from the contactee and not a highly evolved and advanced alien race at all? One answer put forward to this question is that the aliens cannot reveal discoveries or events before they happen, merely warn afterwards. Why, then, has the message changed? There are now more nuclear weapons, more countries with the technology and, with the collapse of the monolithic Soviet empire, the threat of accident has never been greater. The only difference since the end of the cold war is that, perhaps wrongly, we do not perceive the threat as much. It seems the aliens' warnings more closely mirror the concerns of humans (and contactees) rather than the objective situation.

Adamski had great success with his tales of Venusian, Jovian and Saturnian people (they told him that the humanoid form is universal). Unfortunately, subsequent progress in the field of planetary astronomy and space exploration brings into question some of his claims about his visits to the planets. A stroll on the surface of Venus, Saturn or Jupiter would be difficult, particularly since the latter two have no solid surface.

At the time of Adamski's tours the image of Venus was of a sister planet to the Earth. Probes have since shown that, apart from a similar size, the two worlds have little in common. Anyone strolling on the

GEORGE ADAMSKI

George Adamski is noted as being the first contactee with aliens. Contactees are people who claim that they have met, communicated with orally or telepathically and sometimes flown with peoples from other planets.

George and several colleagues decided to go skywatching in the Mojave Desert on 20 November 1952. After a picnic, George was said to have had his first contact with a tall Venusian. All Venusians appeared to have beautiful skin, long hair and wear sandals. The message they told was a simple one, that in the nuclear era that had just been entered, mankind had to be very careful, otherwise they could destroy the fragile planet Earth with radiation. It was a fear shared by most humans at the time (the height of the cold war) so why did Adamski's and subsequent contactees' aliens journey so far to tell people what was already known?

Nowadays, contactees report that the aliens are warning us of global warming, the hole in the ozone layer, and anything else that seems to worry the humans that they contact.

'Hypnosis is often regarded … as a means of retrieving forgotten objective facts …'

surface would have to cope with a carbon dioxide atmosphere (laced with sulphuric acid) at 90 times our Earth's pressure (about the same as 1 kilometre [$\frac{1}{2}$ mile] under the sea) and very high surface temperatures, which makes breathing difficult. It gets worse on Jupiter, where a pressure of 4 million atmospheres above a sea of metallic hydrogen would make sandals rather inadequate. Those that were with George Adamski at the first alien encounter later retracted their stories.

Hypnosis is often regarded by non-practitioners as a means of retrieving forgotten objective facts – a kind of 'truth drug'. Research shows otherwise. Several paranormal associations have conducted experiments with volunteers who are fed either clearly defined fictitious stories or actual experiences that are well documented. Hypnosis is then used to probe the story for detail. In both cases, the result is a highly altered and mostly fictitious tale augmented by material from well-known science fiction.

In fact, what emerges is that it is the type of questions and the way the investigator asks them that have the greater effect on the results. One investigator can elicit a totally different 'reality' from the witness than another. That is why many reputable UFO study groups have banned the use of hypnosis when studying witnesses. The Hills' case started a trend (see 'Betty and Barney Hill, page 46). Out of this arose the whole scenario of alien abduction, usually including medical examination.

· THE TRUE ALIENS ·

Clearly, there are problems with many alien accounts and no physical evidence that would stand up in court. But is an alien visitation really out of the question? What is the likelihood that intelligent life does exist on other planets? Well, it seems increasingly likely that we are not the only inhabited planet.

In 1961 astronomer Dr Frank Drake devised a formula to estimate the likelihood of there being intelligent life in our galaxy. The formula includes such factors as how many suitable stars there are with suitably Earth-like planets orbiting them. The figures in Drake's formula are continually being revised in the light of new discoveries. Some have said that the reasoning behind the formula is flawed, as we know of only one

BETTY AND BARNEY HILL

Betty and Barney Hill were on holiday in Canada when they heard a warning of impending bad weather, so they decided to drive home earlier than planned. While driving down US Highway 3 on 19 September 1961 towards their New Hampshire home, Betty saw a bright light in the distance. At first Barney thought it was a satellite but, using binoculars, he decided it was an aircraft.

They drove on but soon slowed right down when they saw a light circling the car and getting closer. Betty used the binoculars and described a large 'ship' with faces at the windows. They stopped the car and Barney took the binoculars and got out to take a closer look. He described a pancake-shaped craft with the occupants dressed in Nazi uniforms. This panicked Barney and he ran to the car.

On their journey, they had last rested at a diner at about 9pm and arrived home in daylight seven hours later. Betty reported the events of that night and began to read all she could on the subject of UFOs.

Within a week she contacted the National Investigations Committee on Aerial Phenomena, and then started to experience nightmares about all that had happened. It was the investigators, on piecing together the events of that night in September, who discovered that two hours seemed to be missing from their account.

At the Hills' request, Doctor Benjamin Simon conducted hypnotic regression, which resulted in a story of abduction and medical experimentation. To his credit, Dr Simon did not view Betty's collection of writings describing her nightmares until after the sessions and, on comparison, came to the conclusion that Betty was imagining the episodes after a true UFO encounter.

Unfortunately, many hypnotherapists and investigators using this technique to study UFO encounters are not as professional as Dr Simon and give their seal of approval to the events that unfold as if they were genuine memories.

outbreak of life, and that is on this planet. But that is in question, as we seem to share this rock with other different types of life. At school we were taught that all life on Earth needs sunlight to exist. But thermal vents deep down in the oceans seem to have given rise to forms of life that use the Earth's interior heat and a sulphide chemistry rather than traditional sun, oxygen and carbon dioxide chemistry.

So, is this planet unique or our sun special? This planet orbits a second generation star. In the first-generation star, all the exotic metals and elements were formed (the gold, silver and copper in your rings and watches were once at the heart of a star). After its demise, the Earth was blessed with a lot of these elements in comparison to our neighbours. The all-important solvent, water, which was essential for all forms of life, was not present, however, as the young molten-rock planet was too hot. Water arrived on comets, as it did on the other planets and the moon. As soon as the planet cooled enough, life started.

Douglas Adams' *Hitch Hiker's Guide to the Galaxy* got it just right for the Earth, stating that it was 'mostly harmless'. There is not much that marks us out. We are third from the sun, which is an average star in a not very special part of one of the spiral arms in a good-sized spiral galaxy.

New planets are being discovered every few months and, as telescopes and technology improve, this is going to become a weekly or daily occurrence. Planets seem more and more common, and with them the possibility of intelligent life increases. That is why many have actively listened out for life on other worlds. Spacecraft such as Pioneer 10 have carried greeting cards from the inhabitants of Earth to help others understand and find us.

Far from trying to hide our existence, we have from our earliest space flight days broadcast the fact that we are here. Many are participating in the SETI (Search for Extra-Terrestrial Intelligence) project using computers to identify the broadcasts of other beings out there. So, while the chances of being visited by extraterrestrials cannot be ruled out, the evidence presented so far that it has already happened is less than compelling.

'What is the likelihood that intelligent life does exist on other planets?'

STRANGE HAPPENINGS

THESE UNUSUAL PHENOMENA ARE named after Charles Fort, an American researcher who drew attention through his writings in the 1920s and 30s to some of the bizarre oddities that happened in the world. While science has given us reasons for the existence of many things in the Universe, it does not include Fortean phenomena, or natural oddities.

To have any chance of understanding the world, scientists either simplify or look at tiny fragments of it. From these small chunks they then draw conclusions about the way larger and more complicated things work. Fortean phenomena tend to contradict such attempts at understanding. They are the pieces left over from the scientific jigsaw that do not fit. Charles Fort delighted in waving them under scientists' noses.

'Many different events come under the term Fortean phenomena'

• WHAT ARE FORTEAN PHENOMENA? •

Many different events come under the term Fortean phenomena. They include such things as out-of-place animals, for example, a puma in rural England, monsters such as the Loch Ness monster, weeping or bleeding statues – usually religious, religious visions, crop circles, ball lightning, simulacra (things that happen to look like something else), animal and human mutations, fairies, angels, spontaneous human combustion, urban myths, vampires, phantom hitchhikers and conspiracy theories. You could also include oddities in various scientific fields such as archaeology, for example claims of modern items found at ancient sites, meteorology, for example coloured rain, astronomy for example, coloured flashes seen on the moon, biological, for example toads sealed in rocks, and many more.

Obviously, with such a range of phenomena, it is hard to generalize for a paranormal investigator about how they should be investigated.

CROP CIRCLES

Over recent years, crop circles have caught the public's attention. Every summer a kaleidoscope of increasingly bizarre shapes is discovered in fields of agricultural crops. The phenomenon, which started in southern England in about 1980, has spread to many parts of the world, particularly North America, Europe and Australasia.

The regularity of their shape and the crispness of their edges made it apparent that the circles were not caused by wind or rain. A number of exotic theories was produced to account for them, including hedgehogs, UFO landings and earth energies. Meteorologist Terence Meaden suggested that an unusual type of whirlwind was responsible – a plasma vortex – consisting of a descending electrified wind.

But a new set of patterns began to appear, including square boxes and triangles. In 1991, Dave Chorley and Doug Bower of Southampton, England, revealed that they had hoaxed the original crop circles to look like UFO landing marks. They had decided to elaborate the circles further to reveal the hoax and were surprised that they were taken so seriously.

Since then the public seems to have accepted crop circles as hoaxes. But a keen band of researchers are still investigating them, attempting to show that at least some are not.

• CROP CIRCLES
This intriguing shape appeared in a field near Stonehenge, England, in 1996.

You will often need to use your common sense to decide how to proceed. Nevertheless, there are some general principles that can be followed (see Chapter 1, 'Investigating').

A PLAGUE OF FROGS

Many paranormal investigators, when asked what Fortean phenomena are, often mumble vaguely about falls of frogs or fish as being the well-known examples. Recently, such an incident was reported from South London by Phil Walton, a paranormal investigator. He relates the story:

'An elderly lady phoned the local meteorological office and asked if there had been any unusual winds in the area. She went on to say that her lawn was covered with many frogs, but rang off before anybody could take her details. The meteorological office then contacted the local press and several newspapers reported that a Fortean event had indeed occurred, namely a frog fall.'

A closer examination of this statement leads to some curious obser-vations. The lady said that her lawn was covered with frogs. Why not newts, fish or aquatic plants as well? What agent could have lifted frogs out of a nearby pond?

49

FALLING OBJECTS

• Phil would not have been entirely surprised if the frogs had indeed fallen from the sky. He had witnessed a similar event over a decade earlier in nearby Orpington. The town was the victim of a straw fall that covered the entire high street and unsuspecting shoppers with straw from a local farm.

The event made it into the national weather forecast that evening. Phil also came out of work one day only to find his car and many others covered with red sand. Next day the papers were full of the story of the Sahara sand being whisked up by a freak wind into the high atmosphere and deposited over south-east England.

The case of the Croydon woman was very difficult to investigate as the original witness did not leave a name and could not therefore be contacted. Many Fortean cases are similarly short on detail. However, there was enough even in this thin report to come up with some possible explanations. Note, for instance, that the witness did not mention seeing frogs sitting on a roof or in a tree, which might have implied an actual fall from the sky.

Phil Walton runs a gardening business and had seen something similar before. One early spring about five years before, he saw dead frogs on his customers' lawns. While only some of the customers had ponds, what they all did have in common was lots of dead frogs that had apparently been making their way from ponds as if they had become hydrophobic. Listening to a natural history programme on the radio afterwards, he learned of the widespread deaths of frogs caused by a parasite, either viral, bacterial or fungal. Over the years more articles have appeared in the media about these sudden outbreaks that leave whole areas devoid of frogs.

• REPORTED EVENTS •

Fortean researchers gather most of their material from the media. Newspapers and magazines delight in reporting odd events. The *Fortean Times*, the UK-based journal of Fortean researchers, relies on its readers to send in reports from the media. Museums are also a useful source of historical oddities. The Internet is also proving to be a valuable source of strange reports. Sometimes researchers may get reports from a direct source, but this is relatively rare.

The problem with many Fortean reports is illustrated in the frog example given earlier: there is just not enough information available. In the case mentioned there was no witness to interview, so the story could not be followed up. Even if the media do interview witnesses they will often not ask all the questions researchers would like answered.

MEDIA INVOLVEMENT

Usually the media will put a 'spin' on such stories, sometimes taking an openly sceptical stance and gently ridiculing those involved. In other stories they might pursue a particular theory to explain the phenomena without considering the sometimes obvious alternatives. This is because, to achieve popularity, they often pander to the beliefs and stereotypes of popular culture. So stories about ghosts being the returning dead or UFOs being alien spaceships will always get a good readership.

The fact that a story appears in the press does not make it true. This may seem self-evident, but sometimes your instincts are to believe what is in print. Some Fortean stories in the press seem to have unreliable sources, or they have been re-worked.

The origins of unlikely tales fall mainly into three categories: friend-of-a-friend stories (FOAF), urban legends and genuine cases. Unfortunately, it is not always easy to tell one from another. The media does not generally tend to investigate paranormal stories fully, so it is left to Fortean researchers to do it.

• FOAF STORIES •

These stories are given this name because, when asked for the source of a fantastic story, many people will reply that they came from a friend of a friend. The story had been passed in 'Chinese whispers' fashion from person to person, each adding their own 'details' to spice up the story, so that in the end the result bears little relation to the original events.

HOW DO THEY COME ABOUT?

The following story came about in this way. A well-known researcher was approached at a meeting of paranormal enthusiasts to be told of extraordinary events that had been recorded in a reputedly haunted set of show caves in England. Apparently, a team of paranormal investigators had been sent down there and heard and seen all manner of paranormal events. The events really sounded very exciting indeed, the sort of thing all paranormal investigators would give anything to witness. This researcher had heard similar, though less lurid, reports of the same event in the past, and they all made him smile. This was because he had actually been present on the night in question and knew for a fact that the stories were untrue.

This is an example of a typical 'friend-of-a-friend' (FOAF) story. We have all no doubt come across such stories among our own acquaintances, when trivial events have become lurid gossip after a few retellings. The desire to 'spice up' a story is a familiar human trait.

In this particular case the researcher knew the facts and could put the enthusiast right. However, normally these types of stories cannot be so easily traced to their source. It is quite common, on telling someone that

'The fact that a story appears in the press does not make it true.'

STREET LAMP INTERFERENCE

Street lamp interference (SLI) is what happens when an individual seems to cause street lamps to turn off (or sometimes on) without physical contact, as he or she approaches them. Typically a lit street lamp will go off as the person walks by. Obviously this could be a faulty street lamp, in which

• STREET LAMP
'SLIders' have
the unexplained
ability to turn
street lamps off.

case it would probably go off when anyone passed by. However, certain people seem to affect street lamps frequently, far more than faults would suggest. Furthermore, these lamps as unaffected by other passers-by.

At the moment SLI is a phenomenon that it is not officially recognized. Various societies have started to study it, and recently a research project has been started by Dr Richard Wiseman at the University of Hertfordshire in England. However, it is not easy to test for something that happens spontaneously, and which cannot be replicated in the laboratory.

What happens with SLI? It is believed that the 'SLIder' unconsciously performs the physical process of turning off the lamp by remote control. This is not as far-fetched as it sounds. Our brain is a physical electrical instrument, and though the power it uses is very small, we have grown used to the idea that very little power is required to initiate big effects. So SLI could simply be an activity of the brain, transmitting an electrical impulse which happens to have this effect on the switching mechanism of street lamps.

But it isn't that simple. Although this could be the process by which SLI operates, additional factors play a part which may be equally important:

• Many 'SLIders' report being in an unusual mental state.
• 'SLIders' can rarely reproduce the feat deliberately.
• The lamp is affected only by the 'SLIder', not by other people present.
• Many 'SLIders' also report affecting other types of appliance.

Also, many 'SLIders' report other kinds of experience, particularly with electrical appliances. Some claim to affect radios and televisions, others watches and clocks, computers and supermarket check-outs.

It is often commonplace in offices for one person to have a negative relationship with electrical appliances. This is the person who always has problems with computers, who can't wear a wristwatch, and who manages to blow fuses or light bulbs. Many paranormal reports include such cases. The famous Rosenheim 'poltergeist' case involved a young woman who was somehow linked with spontaneous phone calls and interference with the office lighting.

Maybe there is 'a new force' involved in SLI that may be explained as a psychic phenomena. It would probably make sense to study the people affected in the light of the full range of things they affect, since, presumably, the same force is involved whether it's street lamps or computers. However, at the moment, researchers are studying its effect on street lamps.

Summer 1991

'I was walking back from my girlfriend's house after a night out. It was summer time, in the early morning and was quite cold. I was walking though an open park lit by old-fashioned, ornate street lamps, when the nearest lamp post to the footpath went out as I approached. I thought nothing of it except thinking that "the bulb has gone". But the same thing happened the following night, and again I dismissed it as a faulty bulb and thought nothing of it until it happened the next time I passed, at which point I started to think it was unusual.

Over the months as I returned home from my girlfriend's house, the lamp would always do the opposite to its original state, for example, if it was off it would turn on and vice versa. After passing the lamp post it would usually revert to its original state.

It wasn't until I noticed I had the same effect on other lamp posts that I noticed the conditions for the effect to happen. It tended to happen late at night – after 9pm at least. It was normally dark, quite chilly and I was normally tired, on edge and a bit nervous of my surroundings. When I tried to demonstrate to my friends, it would not work as I was probably too relaxed. I can only think the cause of the phenomena is over-active brainwaves, brought about by my nervous state.'

you are interested in the paranormal, to be told that a mysterious 'they' have proved something like alien abductions to be true, or indeed bogus. The mysterious 'they' can invariably never be reliably identified.

'The desire to 'spice up' a story is a familiar human trait.'

• URBAN LEGENDS •

Unlike classic legends, such as those relating to Jason and the Argonauts or Hercules, the urban legends are stories set in thoroughly believable contemporary settings. Instead of involving Greek gods in ancient times, they could have happened to someone you might know, at a place you may have been, recently. They have an important characteristic that differentiates them from the 'genuine' cases (and indeed many FOAFs, which are often based on real cases). They have what folklore researchers call a 'motif'. This is a recurrent 'plot' that occurs, with variations, in all retellings. Though the motif will be set in many different real places at different times, involving different characters, it always remains basically the same. It often has a 'too good to be true' feel about it that should immediately arouse any researcher's suspicions.

WHAT ARE URBAN LEGENDS?

The type of story that is known as an urban legend includes the following: have you ever heard reports of alligators loose in the sewers of New York? Or maybe of someone picking up a hitchhiker on a lonely road at night only for them to disappear later in the journey? Other examples include a story that says you can tell which hemisphere you are in by the way the water rotates when you empty a sink (the effect is real but far too small to be detected outside a laboratory); common emails circulating around the Internet that warn of other virus emails that do not actually exist, and so on.

THE HITCHHIKER LEGEND

The phantom hitchhiker legend is an interesting one. The basic motif is for someone to pick up a hitchhiker, usually on a lonely stretch of road at night. The hitchhiker (often female) is usually reticent. The hiker says she is cold and the driver lends her his coat. At some point later along the road the driver will notice to his great surprise that the hiker has vanished, seemingly from within a closed vehicle. The distraught driver continues on to the next town and reports the incident. He is then told of a terrible accident that happened on that stretch of road. On visiting the grave of the victim he discovers his coat draped over her tombstone.

So what makes this story suspicious? Firstly, it appears regularly in the media in essentially the same form but with different times and locations.

'Fortean researchers gather most of their material from the media.'

There are several recognized variations, but it is essentially the same story. The second point is that it is 'too good to be true'. It is dramatically satisfying, a neatly rounded story with a balanced ending reminiscent of a short story or play.

By comparison, real paranormal cases are messy, usually having no particular structure. A phenomenon arrives for no reason, causes shock and distress to its witnesses and just as mysteriously departs. It is a seemingly random event with no particular meaning for those involved.

THE BLUE BELL HILL GHOST

The ghost mentioned in this story is a 'phantom hitchhiker', but there is an unusual variation where the phantom does not hitch a lift but is actually knocked down. The body is normally never found. But such happenings are supposed to belong to urban legends rather than reality. Some legends are almost certainly based on true incidents, although many of the later elaborations are just added for effect when retelling the story.

In 1966 reports started to circulate in paranormal circles about a hitchhiking ghost that had been seen at Blue Bell Hill near Maidstone in Kent, England. Several reports were collected of drivers who turned up at the Maidstone home of a car accident victim enquiring after a female passenger they had just given a lift to. There were only odd mentions of the ghost over the next few years, but nothing significant happened until 1974, when events marked a change in the phenomenon. A Rochester man was driving home in the early hours of a Saturday morning when he knocked down a young girl who he thought may have been about ten years old. Distraught, he ran back along the road and picked up the girl who was bruised and crying for her mother.

Laying her down by the side of the road, he tried to flag down passing motorists. When no one would stop, he covered her in his car blanket and dashed to the nearest police station for help. When the police arrived at the scene a few minutes later the girl had gone, although the blanket still remained. At first light a full search was conducted of the area with tracker dogs, but no girl was ever found.

Then in 1992 a man was driving home down Blue Bell Hill when he suddenly saw a young girl run straight out from the central reservation in the road in front of him. The amazing thing was that the girl looked him 'right in the eye' before disappearing beneath the wheels of his car. His car skidded to a halt and he searched frantically for the body. He went to Maidstone Police Station to report what had happened and was told of the well-known ghost in the area. No body was ever found. A similar incident also happened a few weeks later.

The motif, by contrast, produces a beautifully crafted story. The motorist is able to identify the hiker easily and even has proof at the graveside. This final flourish, the coat mysteriously transported to the grave, is enough to send shivers down the spine of the most cynical listener. If it really happened.

'Experts may well be highly sceptical of your claims'

HOW IT IS REPORTED

The story is usually told as a FOAF, or is sometimes reported in a newspaper as fact. Details of the time and place add authenticity to the tale. However, if an investigator tries to trace the witnesses involved, they usually cannot be found. Information about the event may be too vague to be able to trace anyone or the witnesses may simply not exist. Such urban legends, fascinating though they are in their own right, are the bane of paranormal researchers in search of solid facts.

However, as in most classic legends and folklore, there is often an incident or incidents that gave rise to these legends. Although the cases of apparently real phantom hitchhikers (see 'The Blue Bell Hill Ghost', page 55) are much rarer and less dramatic than their reports suggest, they do exist. There are some well-attested cases where witnesses can be traced and interviewed. There is sufficient consistency in their stories to make them very credible.

• THE GENUINE CASES •

If a seemingly unlikely case does turn out to be at least partially true, how do you go about investigating it? You should start in the same way as any other case by tracing witnesses and interviewing them, as outlined in detail in Chapter 1, 'Investigating', and also follow these points.

◈ WHAT HAPPENS NEXT?

This depends on the type of phenomenon. With such a diverse field it is very difficult to generalize. However, unless you are an expert in the field involved (for example, astronomy) you would be well advised to talk to someone who is. It is no use pronouncing on the unlikelihood of finding wallabies in the Midlands of England only to be told that zoologists already knew of their certain existence (some in fact escaped from a private zoo in the 1930s and are still reported).

INTERVIEWING WITNESSES

• *This is particularly important with Fortean phenomena as that is often all you have to go on. They tend to be one-offs that your witness may never have seen before and will never see again. These phenomena are rare and haphazard by nature, making their study difficult. But even to have traced a genuine witness is a real achievement in itself.*

◈ WHY DO YOU NEED AN EXPERT?

You need an expert to tell you just how unlikely or otherwise your find really is. There are often rare natural phenomena that may seem extraordinary to non-specialists. Of course, experts may well be highly sceptical of your claims, but most are likely to be intrigued, and they may even offer to help you progress the case.

• PHOTOGRAPHIC ANOMALIES •

Unexpected or puzzling features appearing on photographs seem to be on the increase. Some apparently show objects that were not in view (or at least remembered) when the photograph was taken. These may be ordinary objects, such as an extra person in a group portrait, or more extraordinary ones such as strange coloured streaks or shapes.

The theory you must test first is whether they are normal phenomena. Remember that cameras can go wrong or are not always operated properly. Also, people can forget what they photographed. There is also the possibility of deliberately staged fraud.

Identify exactly what is anomalous about the photograph. Some photographs are supposed to show faces, even though the casual observer would completely fail to find them. If you really cannot see what is unusual, you may need to get the person who gave you the photograph to show you exactly where the anomaly is. In such an instance it is often just a case of the original observer reading too much into a pattern of light, shade and colour.

Just as the full moon seems to look vaguely like a face to the naked eye ('the man in the moon'), so it seems that people think they see 'fairies' in the blades of grass in a lawn. The 'trick' is caused by a tendency of the human brain to look for patterns. More or less random shapes can resemble all sorts of things, including faces, to one person while another sees only blades of grass. The reason the photographer did not see the shape when he took the photograph is due to the fact that still photographs differ quite a lot from reality. Although the scenes appear superficially similar, the human eye is sensitive to a much wider range of light levels than film. So distinct subtle shades of grey may be reduced to a uniformly

• CHURCH GHOST
This photograph revealed a ghostly, hooded figure when it was developed.

• FIGURE IN
CLOUDS
*Taken in
Queensland,
Australia, this
photograph
revealed an
unaccountable
image of the
Virgin and Child
when processed.*

black shape in a photograph. Also, of course, a still photograph freezes the action, allowing us to concentrate on patterns we would not normally notice. This sort of photographic anomaly is very rare with video. As the wind blows grass blades around, the temporary illusory 'figures' will flash in and out of existence.

One thing to look out for with this type of photograph is a source of reflections. A piece of glass – a window, tumbler or mirror, for example – in the field of view of the camera may be all but invisible on the final photograph. It might, however, have a reflection on it that appears to be in the picture. A clue might be a difference in scale, so that a reflected distant object would appear smaller than in real life and look out of scale with any surrounding objects.

• INVESTIGATING PHOTOGRAPHIC ANOMALIES •

Understanding the reasons for strange features on photographs will help you to separate the anomalous from the merely odd. Anomalous photographs can be divided into three main categories:

ACCIDENTAL ANOMALIES

This category is also the most common. The accidental or unintentional creation of an anomalous feature on a photograph probably accounts for the vast majority that are submitted. With a little experience and some basic knowledge of the photographic process it should be possible to recognize these accidents for what they are. Common problems are caused by:

◈ FOCUS

The extreme blurring of something within the camera's field of view can result in a feature with a strange and unrecognizable shape. Auto-focus may result in the highlighting of a feature not identified by the photographer, as the camera locks on to something in front or beyond the subject. Focus-free cameras rely on the deep zone of focus created by a fixed-focus wide angle lens. The subject is sharpest at a reasonable distance from the camera, while closer than this the image becomes blurred and possibly unrecognizable.

◇ VIEWFINDER PROBLEMS

The most common type of amateur camera is the 'compact'. This design uses a direct-vision viewfinder window that does not look through the main camera lens. The person taking the photograph does not see the scene from the same position as the camera lens. It is quite feasible for a large discrepancy to occur between the scene that the person believes they are photographing and that recorded by the camera. The photographer may subsequently express surprise at the appearance of features in the photograph that they believed were missing from the scene in the viewfinder.

Even with a 'single lens reflex' (SLR) camera, where the photographer views the scene through the same lens as the camera, the viewfinder can crop as much as 15 per cent from the view. Another feature of the SLR is the blacking out of the viewfinder when the photograph is taken. This is caused by the mirror swinging clear to allow the light through to the film. This means that the photographer is effectively blind at the moment of the exposure and is unable to see any changes that occur.

It must also be noted that the capacity to 'see what is in front of our eyes' requires a deliberate effort. A professional photographer knows only too well that he needs to scan the scene in the viewfinder to ensure that only the desired subject matter is included in the photograph. Branches and lamp posts growing out of people's heads, the unwanted yellow litter bin in the corner of the otherwise perfect landscape, are examples of the photographer's failure to 'see' what is actually before his eyes.

◇ FLASH

The most popular types of camera have built-in flashguns that operate automatically in low light conditions. Built-in flashes are not very bright and are really only capable of illuminating subjects close to the camera. People with these cameras often think their flash will illuminate vast areas, particularly when they take pictures at large concert venues. Obviously the resulting photograph will be disappointing, showing the back of the head of the person sitting immediately in front, and not much else.

In spite of its limited power, this tiny built-in flash can create some very puzzling pictorial effects. If the photographer is not looking through the camera's main lens he may not notice if objects such as the camera case or strap is right in front. A flash will turn such objects brilliant white as well as out of focus. To anyone not aware of the problem it will look spectacularly bizarre.

'The "trick" is caused by a tendency of the human brain to look for patterns.'

59

◇ FLARE

This shows up as mysterious blotches of light (coloured or white) that appear over the top of the subjects of the picture. It is caused by internal reflections in the camera from a light source just out of shot. It is quite a common fault in amateur photography and can sometimes make a convincing 'anomaly'. Looking at the scene in the photograph, you should be able to deduce where the light sources are – check for shadows cast by objects in the scene.

DELIBERATE ANOMALIES

Features can appear on a photograph that are caused by the deliberate action of the photographer, either for the purpose of deception or as a result of experimentation.

◇ DOUBLE EXPOSURE

Double exposure combines two or more images in one photograph. It can occur in the camera, by accident, or by manipulation in the darkroom. By judicious choice of image and clever manipulation of the relative densities (exposure) of the images it is possible to create a finished photograph that looks authentic.

'Double exposure combines two or more images in one photograph.'

The detection of a deliberate double exposure is very difficult, but examination of the original negatives or transparencies can help when darkroom manipulation has been involved. All the original photographic material that is pertinent to the image under investigation needs to be closely examined. This includes other photographs taken on the same roll of film, especially either side of the image. This will help to identify camera or processing faults, for example, light leaks or fogging. It will also help to give a context for the image. Check if there are other pictures of the same scene, and whether the anomaly manifests itself in other photographs. If not, why not? What was different? How did the circumstances change? Find out if the photographer shows a consistent level of photographic skill.

If the photograph in question is markedly inferior in technical quality to the others, the suspicion must be that there has been a deliberate attempt to hide manipulation. It has become a convention that inferior technique equates to realism, and may be used deliberately to create a documentary feel.

◇ VISUAL TRICKERY

A competent photographer can alter scale and perspective at will by the use of different camera lenses and camera angles.

Photographic perspective can be compressed by using a long lens to bring distant objects closer, while a wide-angle lens can shrink distant objects. Using a low angle can make something appear taller, a high angle will make the same object appear shorter. An impression of movement can be created by using a slow shutter speed, while movement can be frozen with a fast shutter speed. These tech-niques are the normal skills of the professional photographer.

• UFO?
This photograph was produced using double exposure to give the effect of a UFO.

It is possible to create a quite convincing 'UFO' by throwing a car hub cap into the air. After a great many shots with a motor drive on the camera one or two might catch it in such a way as to convince some people. Looking at adjacent negatives would, in this case, however, show up the deliberate trickery. If the photographer refuses to hand them over or mysteriously 'loses' them you can draw your own conclusions.

UNEXPLAINED ANOMALIES

By carefully examining the photographic image and systematically eliminating common errors, it is possible to explain the majority of photographic anomalies. The anomalies that remain are worthy of further study. Use other researchers' knowledge and experience to try and find a rational explanation. Remember that what might be odd to you may be commonplace to someone else.

ANOMALOUS PHOTOGRAPHS

RTIAL WHITIE	These had sharply defined white areas not apparently caused by extraneous light in the camera.
UE AND WHITE ARCS D MISTY PATCHES	The photographs had strange shapes often with striations almost suggesting a vacuum cleaner hose.
TRUSIVE IMAGES	These contained strange objects, such as coloured spheres and in some cases people, that were clearly not present when the photograph was taken.

◇ BEST PRACTICE
Take great care when examining all photographic material to ensure that it is not damaged. Best practice entails handling the material only when absolutely necessary, and only when wearing soft

'Unknown species tend to be found in remote locations.'

cotton gloves of the type designed for this purpose. Store the material in a clean, dry container. Ensure that the photographic evidence is not creased or bent, scratched, dented or allowed to get dusty. If possible, a high quality duplicate should be made to use for most of the investigation process, only referring to the original when necessary. Original photographic material should always be considered irreplaceable and extremely fragile.

In spite of all the possibilities for natural explanations, there are some strange photographs that seem genuinely inexplicable. Dr Vernon Harrison, a past President of the Royal Photographic Society of Great Britain, has examined many anomalous photographs. While he found most had an explanation, there was a small number that did not (see 'Anomalous Photographs', page 61).

• CRYPTOZOOLOGY •

This is the study of 'hidden' animals. It is split into three categories:

◈ **'OUT-OF-PLACE ANIMALS':** These are animals that are simply in the wrong place, for example big cats in Western Europe.

◈ **'UNKNOWN SPECIES':** This category includes animals that could exist but science does not yet accept them, such as the yeti.

◈ **'LEGENDARY ANIMALS':** These are amazing animals such as sea monsters that seem to belong more to legend than real life. They are regularly reported and often draw much media interest.

The average investigator is most likely to come across reports of 'out of place'

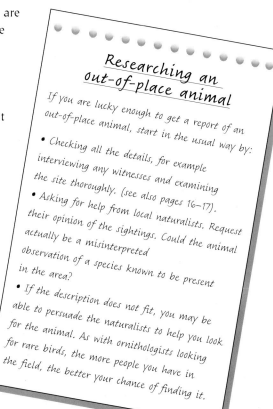

Researching an out-of-place animal

If you are lucky enough to get a report of an out-of-place animal, start in the usual way by:

• Checking all the details, for example interviewing any witnesses and examining the site thoroughly. (see also pages 16–17).

• Asking for help from local naturalists. Request their opinion of the sightings. Could the animal actually be a misinterpreted observation of a species known to be present in the area?

• If the description does not fit, you may be able to persuade the naturalists to help you look for the animal. As with ornithologists looking for rare birds, the more people you have in the field, the better your chance of finding it.

THE ALIEN BIG CAT

This is the name researchers give to 'out-of-place' big cats seen in countries other than their own natural habitat. Alan Cleaver, a paranormal researcher, was living in High Wycombe, England in 1986 when he had the good fortune to see an alien big cat:

'There had been frequent sightings of big cats in the area. Unusually, the police seemed to be well aware that these creatures seemed to have a magical ability of disappearing into thin air. The police went through the motions of sending out armed men to track down the cats sighted through the Chiltern hills but, of course, none was ever found.

And as a researcher and journalist I always carried a camera with me. But when I parked my car outside my home one lunchtime and went indoors I just left the camera in the glove compartment as normal.

It was a bright sunny morning and I stopped momentarily to look out of my one-room flat window. As I looked at the overgrown garden with school playing field behind it, I saw standing right by the steps from the backyard to the garden a big cat!

My first thought was to rationalize that it must be a big domestic cat, a dog or even a fox or some other normal animal that I was misinterpreting. The cat was stood still long enough so that I could examine it closely. It was about 1.1 m (3 ft 6 in) high, tan/brown in colour with a darker face. But what struck me most was its tail, which was long and very thick. The whole animal was well built, giving an appearance of great strength. It sounds almost silly, but I did get the impression that the cat knew I was there and also knew that I did not have my camera on me.

After about five minutes the cat walked off and disappeared into the overgrown garden. There was no evidence, no paw prints were left, no photographs were taken and there were no other witnesses. Strangely I told absolutely no one of my experience for some weeks. I also failed to write down a detailed account straight away. I never bothered to phone the police, even though pupils at the nearby school could have been at risk from a real 'puma' on the loose. Maybe this was because of my embarrassment or part of the phenomenon itself? I wonder how many other witnesses still have not told anyone of their encounter?'

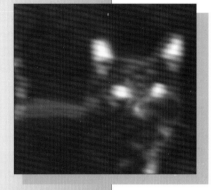

• BIG CAT
Rare sightings have been reported of 'big cats' in southern England.

animals. Unknown species tend to be found in remote locations, for example, a new species of bird was recently found in the rain forests of Ecuador. Legendary animals are often very elusive and are even rarer, making them incredibly difficult to study. People have sought firm evidence of the Loch Ness monster for years with no success.

EARTH MYSTERIES

FASCINATING SITES
FROM THE PAST

THE NAME 'EARTH MYSTERIES', which has been in use since the mid 1970s, is a general term which arose in the 1960s to describe a diverse field of research into the ancient past. Some of the main components are archaeology, astronomy, sacred geometry, folklore, healing, dowsing, ethnography and religious studies. The actual borders of the subject matter are hard to define as they vary for each individual, but the unifying factor is that all the disciplines involved show a respect for ancient culture and the spirit of Gaia (the Earth).

The central focus of Earth mysteries is the study of the prehistoric era – which has a precedent going back at least as far as the antiquarians of the 17th century who laid the foundations of modern archaeology. One of the notable characteristics of Earth mysteries is how intuitive insight has been responsible for many significant discoveries. For instance, we now know from the researches of a Cornish artist that the curious underground Iron Age stone chambers found at Land's End, called fogous, far from having supposedly disorganized plans, in fact have their two entrances facing significant astronomical events.

Another essential ingredient in the field of Earth mysteries is the recognition of the *genius loci* or the 'spirit of place' which haunts many locations. It is this that gives a site its unique quality and it is this that may have suggested the particular configuration of the monument built there.

• PREHISTORIC MONUMENTS •

In about 4,000 BC the people of Britain abandoned their hunter/gatherer existence and settled down to become farmers and pastoralists. This period, known as the Neolithic or New Stone Age, marked a very significant change in the way people lived. Importantly, it saw the erection of the first megaliths and ritual sites. These continued to be built throughout the Bronze and Iron Ages up to the coming of the Romans in AD 43, when prehistory officially ends in Britain.

The legacy of this period is the splendid collection of standing stones, stone circles, burial chambers and earthworks that are to be found all over England, Wales, Ireland and Scotland. Collectively these represent an enormous investment in time and labour. The emphasis of the ancients was clearly on sites constructed for ritual purposes as these were built in stone, whereas the settlements have mostly disappeared.

STONEHENGE
is ancient
onument is
tronomically
gned to the
mmer solstice.

• MYSTERIES •

The word 'mysteries' used in the title refers to the many enigmas relating to these megalithic sites. In many cases their functions are unclear, even if it is supposed that they were built for ritualistic purposes, possibly for promoting fertility. Some plausible scenarios have been suggested, but there are still numerous baffling features to account for.

Some people even speculate that these monuments were designed to harness an energy deriving from the earth or cosmos for the benefit of crops and livestock. One of these enigmatic sites is Silbury Hill, an imposing 45-metre (49-yard) mound near Avebury in Wiltshire, England which covers over 2 hectares (5 acres). It was elaborately constructed in six tiers and inside there are reinforcing walls of hard chalk running radially and concentrically which have kept its shape entirely stable since its construction in around 2750 BC.

Strangely, when it was excavated, the grass beneath was still green and the organic matter inside perfectly preserved. But the question remains why this complex and time-consuming engineering feat was attempted in the first place. No burial area has been found, despite three major excavations, and its function remains a mystery. Another unexplained type of site is the cursus, about four dozen of which have been identified from aerial surveys. They consist of a strip of land about 90-metres (98-yards) wide bounded by shallow banks and ditches. The evidence that has been found shows that ritual activity including feasting took place inside them. Cursuses can be enormously

'The legacy of this period is the splendid collection of standing stones ...'

65

'Over the years dowsing has become an integral part of Earth mysteries.'

long. The Dorset cursus, constructed in a series of straight sections, is some 10 kilometres (6 miles) in length. An essential feature is the long barrows they all have at their beginnings and ends, as well as at articulations and along their length. The barrow seems to be so important that if a genuine barrow was not available a dummy one was constructed, suggesting the cursus may have something to do with ancestor worship or a cult of the dead.

• ASTRONOMY •

It is obvious that the ancients would have understood the changing seasons and appreciated the movements of the heavenly bodies which played such an important part in their lives. This knowledge is often noted in the structures they built. Stonehenge, near Salisbury in Wiltshire, of course, aligns to the rising sun at midsummer, and New Grange in Ireland, an enormous burial mound, has a 20-metre (22-yard) tunnel running to its centre along which the rising sun shines at midwinter. The weather was better at the time most of the monuments were being built, which accounts for the surprising numbers of sites in what are now desolate places like Dartmoor and the north of Scotland. The harvests would have been easier to cultivate and the people probably lived in a harmonious relationship with the earth and her bounty.

Ancient knowledge of the workings of the cosmos can be demonstrated not only in Europe but in civilizations worldwide. The Great Pyramid in Egypt has a long narrow shaft which aligns to a certain star on a significant date in the ancient Egyptian year. More recently, in Central America, the Mayans became fascinated by astronomy and it began to totally control their ritual observances. This is demonstrated by the construction of the Caracol at Chichen Itza – a purpose-built observatory with a very modern appearance.

• DOWSING •

Over the years dowsing has become an integral part of Earth mysteries. It is a method that uses a little understood primary sense that permits the discovery of information that is beyond the capability of the five normal senses. Dowsing is well known for its use in locating water, but it can also find many other things – both

FINDING EARTH ENERGIES

• *Dowsing can also be used to find 'energies'. Research has shown how many ancient sites, such as Stonehenge, have extraordinary earth energy patterns, which many believe induced the ancients to build their ritual centres at such places. There is a general consensus of opinion that ancient monuments were built at particular places to take advantage of concentrations of a natural energy or power, which it is believed could, among other things, enhance any rituals performed there.*

material and non-material. It can, for instance, locate lost objects, buried pipes, oil, metal ores, archaeological remains, as well as date artefacts. It also has a medical application and can be used to diagnose ailments and reveal their cures. In general, it seems to work best when it is asked questions concerning the past or the present rather than the future. In fact, some people like to see it as a way of consulting the 'Akashic Records' (where some believe the knowledge of everything that has ever happened is stored). Others imagine it is governed by some kind of moral law and that it would be impossible to use dowsing for underhand purposes or personal gain.

Dowsing is practised with the aid of an instrument like a forked twig or pendulum. These amplify subliminal muscular movements that are triggered by the brain in accordance with a pre-arranged system of responses. Each individual will have their own set of reactions from a particular instrument.

Dowsers like to rely on a favourite instrument and treat it as if it were an impartial sensing device independent of themselves, which is an excellent way of maintaining the detachment necessary for accurate dowsing. However, using an instrument may make dowsing appear to be more scientific than some of the other divinatory arts, but it must always be remembered that it is nothing more than this.

• CRYSTAL PENDULUM
A small crystal suspended on a fine chain makes an ideal dowsing instrument.

Making an instrument

To make a pendulum

• Suspend a small weight from a fine chain or woven thread (twisted thread may unwind and cause false readings).

• The weight of the bob and the length of the cord may vary but a small weight (100g[3 1/2oz]) on a shorter cord, say 6 cm (2 1/4in), transmits the responses quicker.

To make a pair of 'L' rods

• These can be made from a pair of wire coat hangers. The stiff wire should be about 48 cm (18 in) long. Bend each wire to form a right angle about 15 cm (6 in) from one end.

• TRYING DOWSING YOURSELF •

Nearly everyone can dowse provided they possess an open mind. The distribution of dowsing ability is probably similar to that of any other talent like singing, with exceptional adepts perhaps being rare. It is very easy to have a go as the equipment is inexpensive to buy or it can be made at home. You can use either a pendulum or a pair of 'L' rods. The ancient dowsing tool is the forked twig. Forked twigs can easily break so a good modern-day alternative is two nylon rods bound together at one end, which will work just as well.

'Nearly everyone can dowse provided they possess an open mind'

When held correctly under tension the forked rod exhibits a knife-edge balance which has the advantage of a very positive flip up or flip down reaction. Contrary to popular belief, it is not necessary for instruments to be made out of particular materials. Both types of rods are particularly good for outside work, as they can be used while you are walking about. Dowsing on the move should be down slowly so as not to pass beyond the target spot before the reaction takes place.

A critical factor for success with dowsing is to have a real need to know the answers. Without this you are unlikely to get reliable responses. Another problem to be aware of is fatigue, which will cause your hit rate to tail off fairly quickly. Although the physical effort is admittedly slight, novices need to develop their mental ability before they can dowse for long periods. You should also avoid dowsing when you are off-colour or not able to concentrate well.

USING RODS

When using 'L' rods, hold one in each hand by the short 'arms' with the long section pointing forwards. The standard way of using L' rods is to keep your forearms horizontal with your hands applying just enough pressure to stop the rods swinging about, the long lengths should point slightly downwards, which will also minimize any swaying.

As mentioned, these are good to use outside and when a find is made the usual reaction is for the rods to cross over. It is possible to follow a sinuous line with the rods which will align themselves with its course. A single rod can be used for all these operations if desired.

WITHOUT INSTRUMENTS

With experience you can dowse without an instrument. One way of doing this is to hold your hands in front of you with the palms facing each other about 2 cm (³⁄₄ in) apart. When a reaction occurs the hands will seem to be irresistibly drawn together. One of the marvels of dowsing is that it can be done equally well from a map as on location. This means it is possible to use either a map or a hand-drawn diagram of some area where something has been lost and then to pinpoint its location by remote dowsing. The pendulum is held in one hand in readiness for a reaction while a finger of the other hand explores the paper.

CONDUCTING AN EXPERIMENT

When using a pendulum, the first thing you need to do is to work out your system of responses. This is done simply by asking questions you already know the answers to and then watching to see what the pendulum does, often it will be a gyration in a particular direction. This will quickly tell you what reactions you have for 'yes' and 'no'. Alternatively, you can just ask it 'what is yes' and 'what is no' and see which way it swings. Most people get a clockwise swing for 'yes'.

In certain situations there may be no clear cut answer to a question so you will need to watch out for an indeterminate movement, often swinging backwards and forwards, which will signify your reaction for 'I don't know'. One way of asking questions is to have the pendulum already oscillating, as this imparts energy to the bob and makes it more responsive to minute muscular movements. Having established a system, you will be ready to try out your skill.

❖ Ask a friend to hide coins under a mat or put them in containers for you to identify.

❖ Hold the pendulum over the ground or object and see which way it gyrates.

❖ If you use 'L' rods think deeply about what you are looking for and the rods will cross over when the objects are found.

❖ If you wanted to experiment inside with a forked rod, it would flip up or flip down when the objects are discovered.

ATMOSPHERIC SITES

• *It is widely recognized that stone circles, and other ancient monuments, can be extremely atmospheric places with a profound presence. It is not surprising, therefore, to know that in many cases cathedrals and pre-Reformation churches occupy places of prehistoric worship. This was enforced by the policy of Pope Gregory. In AD 601 he wrote to Bishop Mellitus, who was to join Augustine in his crusade to convert Britain to Christianity, directing that the temples of the old religion were to be sought out and appropriated. Apart from the disposal of the idols and sprinkling of holy water, he dictated that they were to remain in use as formerly, so that the original worshippers might continue to attend and be converted. It is for this reason that many old churches fall on ley lines.*

• DOWSING AND PSI •

Some researchers into the paranormal, such as the late T.C. Lethbridge, made much use of dowsing for their experiments. Lethbridge proposed a theory about seeing ghosts at certain places, whereby moisture and underground streams provided an essential circuit for the recall of what he saw as previously impressed images. The fact that professional water dowsers can sense these streams, suggests a definite connection between these disciplines. Dowsing also appears to use the same sensitivities that are brought into play when practising things like psychometry, telepathy and remote viewing, which have similarities to sensing presences and experiencing ghosts. It is hard to distinguish clear borders between all these disciplines and it is probably true to say that, in the past, when these areas were identified and named, it was more for convenience than anything else. One viewpoint sees all these areas as segments in a continuous spectrum of psychic ability, with all the parts blending into and being interconnected with each other.

• FOLKLORE •

Folklore and personal reminiscences have provided many stories that tell of the strangeness or supernatural influences of ancient sites. The folklore is really delightful as it can often be a repository of profound truths preserved in a symbolic way that makes working them out a pleasant challenge. The central theme throughout is the great respect, almost fear, that is generated by ancient sites. This can make them seem awesome if not daunting places.

This fear is illustrated by the recurring theme of retribution befalling any person who dares to harm them. The folklore will often tell the story of a disrespectful farmer who has stolen a megalith for a farm building rather than take the trouble to search for another stone that might be available locally. Having moved the stone some distance with great difficulty, perhaps using several more horses than expected, the farmer then experiences a series of misfortunes, which eventually convinces him that his best plan is to take the stone back to its original position. This is accomplished with little effort, and his problems immediately cease. Another prominent theme involves the fairies or 'guardians' of a site. These might spirit away an unwary person for a year and a day or otherwise cause enchantment, especially if the site is visited on certain nights of the year.

The existence of these sprites is claimed to be proven by the flitting lights often seen at such places. Researches have shown that all the stone circles in Britain are within 1½ kilometres (1 mile) of a tectonic fault (structural deformation). It has therefore been proposed that the flitting lights were in fact the earth lights of Devereux's theory (see Chapter 3, 'UFOs'). The ancient people when they saw these lights may have believed it indicated a magical spot and accordingly built their major monuments at such places.

' ... it has been claimed that leys transmit an "earth" energy ...'

• LEY LINES •

The curious preponderance of ancient sites falling on straight lines was brought to the public's notice in 1925 with the publication of Alfred Watkins' book *The Old Straight Track*. A few years previously Watkins had experienced what he described as 'a flash of ancestral memory' when the idea came to him while he was examining a map of his local Herefordshire. He gave these straight alignments the name 'ley', which is a Saxon word meaning a clearing in woodland, as he thought these alignments had been originally cut through a densely wooded landscape.

The sort of markers acceptable on a ley would include any of the prehistoric sites so far mentioned as well as traditional springs, hill figures, cross roads, coincident lengths of old track or road, and churches if they are on ancient sites. It is good to have at least four points on a ley, preferably more. Watkins believed leys were laid out in straight lines as an efficient way of transporting essential commodities from one settlement to another.

Hills are often initial points on leys, and he proposed that beacons had been lit on them at night, when they could be seen from great distances, so that markers could be laid out in straight lines before the track was cut. The idea that leys were purely trackways has not stood the test of time as in many cases they follow impractical routes. Since Watkins' day it has been claimed that leys transmit an 'earth' energy, which according to the particular interpretation may be either a good or a bad thing.

It was only some time after the theory of leys was revived by Tony Wedd that the energy connection came about. The end of the 1960s was an inspiring time and many people visited places such as stone circles to find out more about their mystical significance. Some ley researchers currently think that the lines are 'spirit paths'. This is because spirits were commonly thought to travel in straight lines, and many churches or graveyards are approached by straight corpse ways or ghost roads that were used to convey the dead for burial.

> *'It is fun to discover a ley line for yourself.'*

FINDING A LEY LINE

It is fun to discover a ley line for yourself. The impulse to do this often comes from being impressed by a particular site and wanting to see if it is on a ley, but naturally you can check out any site.

◇ SMALL SCALE MAP

Use a small scale map. You will need a larger scale map only if you want to do some in-depth research after finding a ley.

◇ STRAIGHT EDGE

You will also need a straight edge – a transparent rule is excellent. Place the edge of the ruler on the map of the site in question and then slowly revolve it around, watching to see if it crosses any well-known ley sites.

◇ CHECK THE MAP

Go over the map beforehand and circle any potential ley sites in pencil so they are easy to notice. On completion of a 180° degree sweep you may find a number of sites are in line with your target, but it is easy to miss sites so a double check is worthwhile. A ley becomes more convincing as an engineered artefact, the greater the number of sites it has in the shortest distance.

◇ MARK THE MAP

Pencil in the best alignments you have with a thin line and check to see if any can be extended, perhaps onto an adjoining map.

◇ WALK THE LEY LINE

Walk the ley line in the field. This will uncover any additional sites that have not been mapped out, such as small markstones or hilltop notches (i.e. distinctive notches on the skyline).

◇ OTHER EVIDENCE

Other corroborating evidence may be uncovered through archive research. If there is any associated folklore it may tell of a connection between the sites as a distorted folk memory of the alignment.

EARTH CURRENTS

• The Chinese have a centuries-old system called feng shui, which recognizes 'Dragon' earth currents found in mountains and an energy known as ch'i running through the landscape. Their cities, temples, burial places and dwelling places were sited to be in harmony with this energy. A similar sort of system is thought to have existed long ago in northern Europe.

Indeed, there are cultures worldwide which believe there is an all-pervading energy or life-force which animates and breathes life into the planet and its plant and animal life. The Greeks knew it as pneuma, for the Hindus it is prana, for the Pacific Islanders it is mana, the Australian aborigines call it kurunba and the Sioux Indians call it waken. In Europe this life essence has for long been referred to as the 'ether'. In the 19th century the German, Karl von Reichenbach called it odyle and in our own century the Austrian, Wilhelm Reich gave it the name orgone. These few examples show how universal, and how powerful, this theory was.

• EARTH CURRENTS •

If you are interested in practical research there has been an investigation into ancient British sites which has been running for over 20 years. In 1977 a research project was instigated by Paul Devereux, who at the time was editor of a leading Earth mysteries magazine. Having recently taken over the editorship, he was intrigued by the many stories concerning 'energy' that were associated with ancient monuments, so he asked his readership to send in what information they had, especially if they thought they had proof of this elusive earth energy.

It subsequently became clear that although the anecdotes were prolific and the idea of an energy was widely accepted, there was little in the way of hard evidence to substantiate its existence. The next move was to call a meeting in London to which Earth mysteries researchers, sensitives, artists, engineers and scientists were invited. The idea was to form a wide-ranging group to do practical research in the field and check whether there was any correlation between what the psychics and dowsers claimed and what scientific instruments could pick up.

THE DRAGON PROJECT

The investigation was named The Dragon Project after the Chinese earth currents used in feng shui, and the researchers who were involved established a base at the Rollright stone circle in Oxfordshire, the nearest stone circle to London, which has the additional attraction of having a burial chamber and a standing stone located nearby. There are, of course, no instruments which can directly monitor these earth energies, at least not to date, so it was necessary to use conventional equipment in the hope that some secondary effects might register on them.

- ◆ Ultrasound, which is a high-pitched sound, above human hearing, that is used by bats. In fact, it was a naturalist who first noticed ultrasound emanating from a megalithic site at dawn while he was returning home after a night's bat hunting. The device to test for ultrasound was fortunately inexpensive, and this encouragingly gave positive responses on a number of occasions, which was an auspicious start.

- ◆ Another fascinating area of research was the testing of dowsers while they were at work, using a machine called a mind mirror which indicates changes in brain waves.

It is not possible to tell the whole story, but over the years the Dragon Project has discovered anomalies in magnetism, radioactivity, infrared photography and other areas on numerous occasions at sites all over Britain. This work continues on many fronts, including, more recently, the recording of dreams induced by particular sites, and there are still opportunities to take part in this monitoring work for people who are interested.

REMOTE VIEWING

TRAVELS OF
THE MIND

I
N THE STRANGE AND WONDERFUL world of anomaly research, one of the current buzz words is remote viewing (RV). But what exactly is remote viewing? According to physicist and RV researcher Russell Targ, 'it is the capacity of people to describe remote locations and events accurately through channels of perception'. Put more simply, it is a way of obtaining information by a method that does not rely on our usual five senses. One form of RV involves a 'sender' and a 'receiver', with the sender trying to transmit impressions to the receiver – a type of telepathy. Another form involves a 'receiver' on his or her own trying to form impressions of a place remotely, without anyone 'sending' anything.

> **'One form
> of RV involves
> a "sender"
> and a
> "receiver" ...'**

The term, remote viewing, was actually only invented in 1972 by researchers at Stanford Research International (SRI), Menlo Park, California. Paranormal investigators are unlikely to come across many spontaneous cases of remote viewing. However, they might find it highly instructive to try out for themselves as it involves many useful principles of paranormal research.

The first controlled RV experiment was written about as early as 550 BC. The writer, Herodotus, describes how King Croesus, who was concerned about the build-up of Persian forces around him, decided to send scribes to various oracles around Greece and Lydia. One hundred days after they left, the scribes were to ask the oracles what the King would be doing on that particular day. After writing down the oracles' utterances the scribes then returned to the King and gave him their writings.

After reading what had been said at Delphi, the King proclaimed that the Delphic oracle was correct. The scribes had copied down the following verse:

> *'I can count the sands and I can count the oceans.*
> *I have ears for the silent, and know what the dumb man nameth;*

Lo! On my sense there striketh the smell of a shell-covered tortoise.
Boiling now on a fire, with the flesh of a lamb, in a cauldron.
Brass is the vessel below and brass is the cover above it.'

Not quite what modern researchers might use as a target! However, when you know that on the hundredth day after the scribes had left, the King took a tortoise and a lamb and cooked them in a brass pot with a brass lid, it becomes very impressive indeed!

'The first controlled RV experiment was written about as early as 550 BC.'

• MORE RECENT EXPERIMENTS •

In the 1920s, psi (psychic phenomena) researcher, Upton Sinclair, and his wife, Mary Craig Sinclair, conducted more than 100 experiments in which Upton Sinclair would draw a picture and his wife would replicate the drawing without seeing it. What Mr Sinclair found was that his wife would sometimes draw the image correctly but then incorrectly identify it. The other phenomenon that occurred in these experiments was that sometimes Mary Craig would draw images that were not drawn on the original, but which Sinclair had been thinking about just prior to the experiment.

• SOME RECENT UK EXPERIMENTS •

RV research has been conducted as part of an on-going series of experiments carried out from 1981 to the present day by the UK-based research association, ASSAP (see page 144). Obviously, many experiments do not score at all well, but one that produced a good hit was a session conducted by Clive Seymour for ASSAP on 22 September 1996. A target pool of pre-selected sites was set up. Each address was placed in a separate envelope and shuffled and then numbered. From this pool, envelope number 11 was chosen and the sender was dispatched. Once alone, the sender opened the envelope and made his way to the named target site. Once there the sender spent some time trying to interact with the place, keeping his focus on the target area (this is not as easy as it sounds) and made his own notes about the place before leaving.

FLYING HIGH

• *The late Michael Bentine CBE also used remote viewing. During World War 2 he was a RAF Intelligence Officer who, after briefing bombing crews and watching the Lancasters and Halifaxes fly off, would retire to the quiet and relative comfort of the operations room and go into a light trance. He would scan with his mind until he could feel the bitter cold of the aircraft, the steady hum of the engines and the quiet, earnest talk of the Polish aircrew, and for the next six hours he would be 'flying' with them.*

EXTRA-SENSORY ESPIONAGE

If you think that remote viewing is little more than an intriguing party game, think again! It has attracted the attention of the US military and intelligence organizations at the very highest level, and it has been estimated that between 1973 and 1995, the American government spent approximately $20 million on RV funding. But why should the US government have spent this amount of money? The answer is simple: fear.

From as early as the 1920s through to the 1970s, many impressive examples of paranormal research were conducted behind the Iron Curtain. Many of these experiments were of a scientific nature. Some, however, had far more sinister implications – including one experiment where it was possible for a man to alter the heart rate of an unknowing subject. If it was perfected, RV could become a vital weapon in military intelligence. It would provide information about inaccessible targets much more cheaply, and in far greater detail, than satellites could. It would become possible to 'see' secret missile bases, spot new submarines, and look inside biological weapon factories.

In the 1960s, rumours reached the West that as many as twenty Soviet universities were conducting ESP research and that the Soviet government had spent $15 million on psychical research. This was at the height of the cold war, when memories of the Cuban missile crisis were still fresh in the minds of those at the Pentagon. The US military had no option but to take the threat seriously. The known history of the US military and intelligence organizations' involvement

with remote viewing began in 1973, with SCANATE. The idea was to supply a latitude and longitude to an RV subject, who would then describe what was there. Early experiments proved convincing enough for the CIA to provide funding. The CIA supplied the co-ordinates (including targets to which the public had no access) and confirmed the accuracy, or otherwise, of the experiments.

Subsequent military-funded studies of RV were: Grill Flame (1978–83), Center Lane (1983–86), Sun Streak (1986–91), and finally Star Gate (1991–95). Joseph McMoneagle, an intelligence officer who took part in Star Gate, described publicly some striking successes. For instance, he drew an extraordinarily accurate picture of a wind-powered electricity generator plant. The only prior information he had was that an unknown person would be looking at an undisclosed scene at a given time somewhere in the continental United States. McMoneagle claims this success was by no means unusual.

There is considerable controversy over these studies. Much of the material remans classified. A CIA report, requested by the US Congress, concluded that results did not justify the continued use of remote viewing in intelligence gathering and brought about the closure of Star Gate. However, the report has been criticized by professional parapsychologists as well as by those who took part in the project. Dr Jessica Utts, a statistician who helped compile the report, was strongly critical of the methods used to research it and disagreed with its conclusions.

'The results ranged from descriptions of tall tower blocks to peaceful, rural scenes of green fields ...'

This experiment was a postal session for people all over the United Kingdom to try to focus in at a pre-arranged time, and in the days that followed about 100 replies came in. The results ranged from descriptions of tall tower blocks to peaceful, rural scenes of green fields, with trees and cows (something sadly lacking in London!). A good proportion of the results were found to contain at least one of the key elements of the target. However, there was a direct hit sent in by an ASSAP member, Roy Maidment of West Sussex, who correctly viewed three of the four key elements of the site:

◇ A river.

◇ Street lamps, including the correct number of them.

◇ A bridge.

◇ He did not identify the fourth key element, that of a group of satellite dishes.

• SIMPLE SHAPES
When selecting target sites for RV experiments, choose buildings with simple shapes, such as skyscrapers.

On another occasion Roy Maidment also managed, in the middle of an RV session, to correctly follow the sender in his mind, accompanying him as he drove his car, turning left and right until finally reaching the target site. The description that Mr Maidment gave of this was later confirmed by the sender on his return to base.

. you have to work at RV in order to develop our skills.'

MIXED SUCCESS

Clive Seymour's personal success with RV has been variable. In another experiment he wrote down that he could see from above a pier running out into the blue sea. In fact the target turned out to be the famous Telecom Tower in central London viewed with a blue sky in the background. A case of the right image, the wrong interpretation!

This is a classic example of the rational mind trying to fit what is 'seen' into a known landmark. The first image is often the best.

In order to expand the numbers of people taking part in RV sessions, research has been conducted with the help of newspapers and magazines and sessions have also been undertaken on the Internet on the association's web site. Anyone can take part in such experiments.

• BASIC REMOTE VIEWING EXPERIMENT •

As with any talent, you have to work at RV in order to develop your skills. You need practice, dedication, patience and a total belief in your ability to remote view. When you are remote viewing, remember that 'remote sensing' is a more apt description of what you are doing. You may not 'see' an image as if you were looking at a TV screen. The subconscious mind tries to transmit images and representations to us, but our rational mind tries to dominate the more intuitive side and browbeat this information.

Very often the first image(s) received are the most important. We nearly always go wrong when we try to analyze and interpret the results. This is why it is a good idea to allow someone else to write down your commentary or, if no one else is available, to record your images and impressions using a tape recorder. This will help prevent you judging what you are 'seeing'. The rational, logical part of you can come back into play once you have stepped back over the threshold and closed the door!

'Very often the first images received are the most important.'

SIMPLE BREATHING EXERCISE

Breathe deeply and slowly and focus your attention on your feet. Breathe in, hold your breath and clench your toes. As you breathe out unclench your toes and relax your feet. Now breathe in slowly and again hold your breath, but this time tense the muscles in your lower leg and then relax them as you breathe out again. Keep this routine up until you have focused on and relaxed all parts of your body. Any book on hypnosis or meditation should contain similar exercises.

You also need to clear your mind, so try visualizing that you are walking into a special room that has a very comfortable chair for you to sit in, and that the only time you visit this room is when you are about to commence an RV session. Make the room as real as you can. The shape and decor is for you to choose. Some people may visualize that they are changing their ordinary clothes for something else. Recommended relaxation music can also help to calm you both mentally and physically.

PREPARATION

◇ Wear loose comfortable clothes.

◇ Do not start a session when you have just eaten or you are hungry. Hunger and the digestive process may affect your ability to relax.

◇ Select a quiet room where you won't be disturbed.

◈ If you are the viewer, use the bathroom before you start – remember you are trying to achieve a relaxed state!

◈ Take the telephone off the hook to avoid any disruptive interruptions.

◈ Dim the lights – remember you are trying to create an atmosphere of calm where your mind won't flit from one thought to another.

◈ Before the session, try to learn a simple breathing exercise such as the one given below. It will help relax your body and begin to affect your state of consciousness.

◈ Once your body is relaxed, try to calm and still your mind.

TYPES OF REMOTE VIEWING EXPERIMENTS

SECOND PERSON RV
This is the basic RV experiment, in which person A acts as the viewer and person B visits the target site and 'sends' impressions to person A.

COORDINATE RV
The viewer is given map coordinates in degrees, minutes and seconds and uses these as a way of locking into the target. This technique was developed by Ingo Swann at SRI and became known as SCANATE or scanning by coordinates.

PHOTOGRAPHIC RV
A photograph which has a strong visual image is placed in an envelope and given a random six-digit number. This number is used by the viewer as a focus for 'seeing' the image. One obvious advantage of this type of RV is that you are not restricted to your surrounding area, rather the whole world and beyond becomes accessible. Also you do not need to know how to read maps!

... "remote sensing" would be a more apt description ...'

CONDUCTING THE EXPERIMENT

You will need people to select the sites, people to visit these sites and act as senders, and also the all-important people, the viewers – together with an independent arbiter or judge. Rotate everyone around so that each person gets a chance to try the different tasks.

◈ SELECT A POOL OF 20 TARGET SITES

These sites should be selected by someone who is unconnected with the RV session. The details of each site – directions, map references, key features, landmarks – should be written on a card, and each card placed in an opaque envelope, which is then sealed. Each site should consist of features that are visually strong and unique, such as buildings with a bold, simple shape.

◇ SELECT ONE ENVELOPE TO USE AS THE MAIN TARGET SITE
The envelope should be selected at random by an impartial observer and given to the sender.

◇ AGREE A START AND FINISH TIME

◇ OPEN THE ENVELOPE
When he or she is alone and out of sight of the viewer, the sender should open the envelope. The sender should then go to the target site and wait for the appointed time.

◇ AT THE APPOINTED TIME, BEGIN THE EXPERIMENT
The sender should concentrate on transmitting impressions of the site to the receiver.

'The true breakthrough will be when we understand the process of remote viewing.'

◇ MAKE NOTES AND SKETCHES
The sender should make notes and sketches of the target site before leaving. At the same time, the viewer should write down and/or draw what he or she can sense.

◇ SIGN AND DATE NOTES
Prior to the sender's return, the viewer shall finish his or her notes and sign and date them. These should then be handed to another person.

◇ MAKE SURE THERE IS NO FEEDBACK
No feedback should take place until all the notes have been signed, dated and given to another person.

Any judge used must be an independent person with no other connection to the sessions. The judge shall be given the target site envelope plus any four of the other envelopes in the target pool to act as controls. The judge must not know which envelope contains the actual target site. He or she will be asked to compare the description and/or sketches given by the viewer with that of the target site, and judge which is the most accurate.

• THE FUTURE OF RV •

Remote viewing has come a long way since it was used by shamans who were in tune with the subtle ways in which nature works. There is now good, solid evidence published in many prestigious journals from many research centres and universities throughout the world. Many former US government remote viewers now run workshops on remote viewing for different industries.

The true breakthrough will come when we understand the process of remote viewing. If we look at the weight of evidence and accept that it works, then the logical step is to find out how it works. We will take a large step forward when physicists begin to unravel the complex sub-article world of quantum mechanics.

Another exciting prospect is to use remote viewing to visit distant planets or galaxies, and possibly revisit the past. In fact, some of these types of uses have already been tried. We are hampered only by our lack of imagination, so it is now time to rediscover this gift for yourself.

COINCIDENCES

THE SYNCHRONICITY OF EVENTS

I T MAY SEEM HARD TO understand why a paranormal investigator should look into cases that involve coincidences. A coincidence is, after all, just an incident that happens through blind chance. But this coincidence may have a real significance to the people involved. Also the coincidence could be so unlikely that it seems to have a significance all of its own. Sometimes coincidences keep happening to one person, seemingly for no apparent reason. Clearly, in these cases, there is a possibility that something paranormal may be involved so are worthy of investigation.

• MEANINGFUL COINCIDENCES •

One of the fathers of modern psychology, Carl Jung, took an abiding interest in what he termed 'synchronicity' – coincidences that were so meaningful that the odds against them happening by chance seemed very high. In fact he recorded one of his own experiences in *The Structure and Dynamics of the Psyche; Collected Works*:

'A young woman patient had, at a critical moment in analysis, a dream in which she was given a golden scarab beetle. While she was telling me this I sat with my back to the closed window. Suddenly, I heard a noise behind me, like a gentle tapping, and saw a flying insect knocking against the window pane from outside. I opened the window and caught the creature in the air as it flew in. It was the nearest analogy to a golden scarab that one finds in our latitudes, a scarabeid beetle, the common rose-chafer, which contrary to its usual habits had evidently felt an urge to get into a dark room at this particular moment.'

For Jung there were many aspects to this synchronicity. The scarab was a classical re-birth symbol. He felt its 'urge' to enter the room coincided with the critical turning point of the patient and the other

'Sometimes coincidences keep happening to one person ...'

82

content of her dreams. It also fitted so neatly with his own theory of 'archetypes' – messengers from the collective unconscious presenting themselves through their own symbols'.

Several researchers in the past century have compiled lists of coincidences. One of the earliest was Alice Johnson, secretary of the newly formed Society for Psychical Research in the 1880s. She had to

! EXTRAORDINARY COINCIDENCES

Some coincidences do not seem to be particularly meaningful to those involved. However, the odds against their happening is incredibly high. Consider the following example.

In 1967 the Reverend Dr Norman Cockburn agreed to show the sights of London to a Canadian couple, Beth and Bill Purves, who were friends of his cousin in Ontario. Lunching near St Paul's Cathedral, he remarked how a neighbour of his at New Malden, Surrey, Mrs Widdup, claimed she had never visited St Paul's, despite being only ten miles away. The guests asked whether Norman had stayed anywhere else in Canada, apart from with his cousin. He replied that he had stayed with a Presbyterian minister friend called Stuart Johnston who was from Montreal.

Beth Purves then said, 'It's very good of you finding time at such short notice, but today was the only day we could fix as we are off to Northern Ireland. Bill has friends there. You don't happen to know a place called Green Island do you?' 'Why yes,' Norman responded, 'I often stay there with a close friend and his family - Jim McDonald'.

Inside the cathedral they brushed past two ladies, one of whom lifted her head

and said with astonishment: 'I thought I recognized your voice, Dr Cockburn, I'm paying my first visit to St Paul's Cathedral!' It was Mrs Widdup of New Malden.

The group then crossed the road to the tourist information office, where two visitors were just leaving. Incredibly they were Jim McDonald and his wife from Green Island in Northern Ireland.

The last visit of the afternoon was to the Tower of London, where Dr Cockburn commented: 'Now just let me take you to the Traitor's Gate before we leave.' There, a large party of Canadians was being guided around. Suddenly, their leader, a minister, turned round and exclaimed, 'Well, Norman, how amazing meeting you here.' It was Stuart Johnston of Montreal!

Here there was no particular significance in the events to the participants, but if such a coincidence against similarly unlikely odds occurred in an experiment a scientist may well conclude there was some significance to it, especially if it was repeated.

From *The Challenge of Chance* by Sir Alister Hardy, Robert Harvie and Arthur Koestler contend with hundreds of reports which might attract other labels today, they included:

◇ A dying person appearing to a close relative.
◇ The weights of a large clock crashing at the time of someone's death.
◇ Future events being foretold through dreams.

• SERIALITY •

'Serendipity – the faculty of making agreeable or useful discoveries apparently by accident ...'

While coincidences seem to occur in many different ways, one particular type seems to happen particularly frequently. Austrian biologist Paul Kammerer, in 1900, was impressed by innumerable trivial examples, that came about time and time again. Many people may have travelled on a Number 9 bus to the theatre, to end up sitting in Seat 9, Row 9, and been given a cloakroom ticket that was numbered 000009. Kammerer dubbed such coincidental events as 'seriality'.

• LUCKY AND UNLUCKY PEOPLE •

Sometimes coincidences seem to happen constantly to the same person. This would certainly be of interest to a researcher because it implies that there is a definite phenomenon at work. One manifestation of this is people who are accident prone. Some people, apparently through no fault of their own, seem to be subject to far more than their fair share of bad luck.

Wolfgang Pauli, whose Uncertainty Principle is one of the cornerstones of modern physics, suffered all his life from what seemed to be a personal 'poltergeist'. Something always seemed to break in a laboratory the moment he stepped through the door. It was so well known and predictable that colleagues named it the 'Pauli Effect'.

Equally, some people seem to be extraordinarily lucky in everything they do. Brian Inglis considers that intuition – arriving at decisions or conclusions without explicit or conscious processes of reasoned thinking – might explain 'lucky' coincidences. Serendipity – the faculty of making agreeable or useful discoveries apparently by accident, but in a way that suggests guidance – could also be invoked to explain the activities of 'library angels'.

LIBRARY ANGELS

• *Researching the Nuremberg war-crime trials at a specialist library, Dame Rebecca West was horrified to find the information abstracted and catalogued under useless arbitrary headings. After hours of searching for a particular event she went along the line of shelves to an assistant librarian and said: 'I can't find it, there's no clue, it may be in any of these volumes.' 'I then put my hand on one volume, took it out and carelessly looked at it. Not only was it the right volume, but I had opened it at the right page.'* (from: The Challenge of Chance, *Sir Alister Hardy, Robert Harvie and Arthur Koestler*).

Both types of incident may invoke a similar unconscious mechanism. The successful scientist may have five options to consider, but really doesn't know where to start. The final choice, however, may not be random: his unconscious mind, having done its homework in advance, nudges consciousness towards the most likely winner. Similarly, the misfit deep down is being guided towards his next tragic encounter and its pay-off – sympathy from all around him. Arthur Koestler suspected another contrarian benefit, with which Carl Jung might agree:

'When major and minor calamities crowd together in a short span of time, they seem to express a symbolic warning, as if some mute power were tugging at your sleeve. It is then up to you to decipher the meaning of the inchoate (original) message. If you ignore it, nothing will probably happen; but you may have missed a chance to remake your life, have passed a potential turning point without noticing it. It is not altogether a naive superstition that such series are often produced by unconscious arrangement' (from *Arrow in the Blue*, Arthur Koestler).

• WHAT IS A COINCIDENCE? •

Perhaps a good working definition of coincidence is what Kammerer described as: the lawful recurrence of the same or similar things and events. A recurrence or clustering, in time or space, whereby the individual members of the sequence, as far as can be ascertained, are not connected by the same active cause.

But quite how lawful are these? First we must assess a number of possible criticisms, and then look at the very nature of chance itself:

◈ Prior knowledge is an obvious candidate for scrutiny, whether conscious, or otherwise. The latter crops up often in paranormal research in the guise of 'cryptomnesia', literally 'hidden memory', which suggests that everything we see, do or experience is recorded in our unconscious mind.

◈ Selective memory is another concern. An instructive, simple exercise is to record how many times in a year we just happen to notice a full moon in a cloudless sky.

◈ Most fundamentally, we should check our sources of information, as far back as possible. How reliable are they? Seasoned paranormal researchers recognize immediately what Arthur Koestler called the 'inkfish effect'. Many cases are quoted and requoted in successive books, yet tracing the original account

'Maybe coincidences are happening around us all the time ...'

85

'... accounts are often embroidered with successive re-telling.'

finds obstacles. Diaries are lost, memories differ, eye-witnesses die or disappear suddenly, official reports are 'relocated' never to appear again. And of course, accounts are often embroidered with successive re-telling.

◇ Also we need to ask whether coincidences are really that uncommon. Often when we are about to buy a car we focus on a particular model, an unusual one perhaps. Then suddenly we see them everywhere. Maybe coincidences are happening around us all the time, but we just don't notice them. Indeed, there is evidence to suggest that we may have to be in an 'altered state of consciousness' such as a light meditative trance to observe coincidences better. Or perhaps even cause them?

The French mathematician Laplace stated that too often, insufficient consideration was given to the greater number of non-coincidences which have made no impression, or which are unknown. How often do we think of a relative, when we do not receive a phone call or letter. Or how often do we not have a vision of someone's demise?

Nevertheless, the coincidences that do make an impression have to be looked at seriously.

• CHANCE HAPPENINGS •

Since chance is so commonly invoked as an 'explanation' of what coincidence is, it needs to be examined more closely:

◇ If you tossed a coin a million times, the total number of heads expected by chance would be exactly 50 per cent.

◇ Guessing tests with five-symbol Zener cards are described in Chapter 8, ('Are you psychic?'), and here chance expectation in a very long run of guesses would be exactly 20 per cent.

But along the line are patches often having very significant deviations from chance. Some guessers have produced scores with odds against chance of 10 to the power 27 (10 followed by 27 noughts!)

AGAINST THE ODDS

• *While there have been hints of lax experimental protocol with card guessing that might allow cheating or sensory clues, it is hard to fault the results of Dr Helmut Schmidt in the 1970s. His subjects were faced with four coloured lamps lit in a random sequence governed by a radioactive source (which the laws of physics say should be completely random). They had to guess which of the four lamps would light up next and press a button corresponding to it.*

In a series of 74,000 guesses, three subjects made 900 more correct ones than would be expected by chance, which translates to odds of ten thousand million to one.

During the autumn of 1967, for seven Monday evenings, 200 people met in London's Caxton Hall to undertake a classic series of experiments arranged by the eminent biologist, Professor Sir Alister Hardy. The original idea was to investigate the possibility of telepathy in a particular way, but unexpected 'simultaneous coincident thoughts' quite unconnected with the test material kept emerging from the participants. With colleague Robert Harvie, Hardy devised a series of unprecedented tests leading to startling conclusions. Coincidences in rigid control tests were as striking as those in the original experiment and convinced them that telepathy, even if it played a part, was not the whole story.

'... randomness may not be as random as we assume.'

These results caused Harvie to experiment with chance itself. Some 25,000 random digits were prepared by colleagues with computers:

◇ The numbers were then arranged in tables, 10 rows by 10 columns wide.

◇ These tables were then compared with tables of the same size from random number tables and examined to see whether any digits appeared in the same position in 'source' and 'target' blocks. Chance expectation of this would be 1 in 10.

◇ Overall, Harvie found considerably fewer than chance might predict. Odds of 62 to 1 against chance in fact, and in some blocks the deviation from chance entailed odds of 1,250 to 1. While these figures are respectably low compared with the astronomical scores obtained occasionally by talented card guessers, Harvie was led to conclude that randomness may not be as random as we assume.

Cambridge mathematician, George Spencer Brown had published an heretical thought some 17 years earlier in the science journal *Nature*, suggesting that while the results of many card-guessing tests runs were significantly above chance, overall they were not spectacularly so, given the decline effect, and that the scores dropped eventually to chance level. Rather controversially he claimed that the apparent success of ESP experiments was really the failure of probability theory applying to reality.

RESEARCH INTO CHANCE EVENTS

Research by Dr Stewart Kauffman at the Massachussets Institute of Technology in the USA suggests the well-known 'order from disorder principle' – which may govern life itself – could result from a curious non-random quirk of probability at a fundamental level. He studied the behaviour of randomly constructed systems, or 'nets', of binary elements. These nets, simulated by computer, consisted of elements like switches, each of which could be in an on or off position.

87

'The universe begins to look more like a great thought than a great machine.'

Sir James Jeans

For a net of 2,000 elements, the number of possible states is huge – 10 to power 602 – and we might logically expect a net system kicked arbitrarily into action to cycle randomly through all these possible states. In fact, Kauffman found a surprising degree of order, the system actually tended to cycle through a very small number of states. And if a system were disturbed from this equilibrium, it returned to the same cycle of states in 90 per cent of all cases.

Whereas classical Newtonian physics would expect random events to be spaced evenly, modern chaos theory lends support to the observation of 'clustering', which is actually more probable. As we start looking at sub-atomic levels, probability becomes paramount. Indeed, quantum theory and the whole edifice of modern physics depends crucially upon it. No longer are the primary particles of matter like hard miniature billiard balls fixed in position; rather they have the properties of waves spreading through the universe of time and space. An electron cannot now be pinned down at a given place – all we can know is the odds or probability of its being there.

In *The Challenge of Chance*, Sir Alister Hardy, Robert Harvie and Arthur Koestler state that: 'The laws of probability describe how a collection of single random events can add up to a large-scale certainty, but not why. Why do not the million nuclei explode at once? Why should we expect that a symmetrically balanced penny will not fall 'heads' on during every toss from now to eternity? The 'order from disorder' principle seems to be irreducible, inexplicably "just there"'.

Many eminent physicists assumed there must be something beyond and beneath the sub-atomic world to account for such apparently indeterminate processes. This 'hidden variables' theory, which enforces the laws of probability 'secretly', failed to find general acceptance through lack of evidence. But in 1973, Evan Harris Walker developed a theory in which the 'hidden variables' were identified with consciousness as 'non-physical but real entities connected to the physical world by the quantum mechanical wave function'.

For centuries, mystics and philosophers maintained that mind or consciousness were central to the workings of the universe, but the arrival of the new physics brought it into sharper focus. Sir Arthur Eddington said in 1927 that: 'The stuff of the world is mind stuff. The stream of knowledge is heading towards a non-mechanical reality.'

• CAN WE CAUSE COINCIDENCES? •

In *An Experiment with Time*, first published in 1927, John W. Dunne presented research into his own dreams, which he recorded on waking.

Some of these dreams were dramatic, others rather mundane, but then he encountered the events, either personally or through the news, very shortly after the dreams occurred – usually on the same day. He claimed no psychic faculty in the traditional sense, but neither did he believe it was chance coincidence. Dunne felt his observations resulted from a small displacement in time which should be accounted for within the framework of physics.

Coincidence, of course happens, as in the event described below. But like John Dunne's experience, was it precognition, a small time slip, or did it just occur because I was pre-occupied with the subject and then somehow manage to 'cause' the event? It would not be the first time. As a teenager in the 1950s, the following was one of several I engineered consciously and deliberately.

The family had arranged a summer holiday in London, and as a change from car driving, we had booked to travel from Swansea by coach. As a transport enthusiast, it was vitally important for me to have a front seat to observe the fullest detail of this annual exploration, but seats were not reservable. For six months I 'worked' on it.

That August morning, Swansea coach station was a seething mass of chaos. Hundreds of people were already queuing for London as a string of coaches, old and new, arrived. Slowly they filled up, and with half-a-dozen people still ahead of us, we awaited the next arrival. Suddenly, an inspector called the six in front of us forward to fill spaces on the front vehicles, and simultaneously a brand-new coach swung in. The best seats and excellent views were ours. So how did this happen? Maybe it occurred because of my 'faith' that it would happen.

Coincidence?

I was driving along the winding road from Frome to Bath in Somerset, England. As a lorry labelled 'HTS Logistics' (I think) passed me, I bemoaned the current welter of instantly forgettable initials. Far better, I felt, would be a simple but unusual name. Ptarmigan came to mind. No, that was too difficult to spell. Perhaps Eagle? No, rather overused. Kestrel? Yes, Kestrel would be an excellent choice. Ten seconds later, round the bend came a lorry that was emblazoned "Kestrel Packaging".'

'The first priority is to make sure you have all the facts of the case.'

• INVESTIGATING COINCIDENCES •

When you come to investigate events involving coincidences, it will be very similar to investigating premonitions (see Chapter 11, 'Premonitions'). The first priority is to make sure you have all the facts of the case. You should interview the witnesses to check that the incident really did take place as reported. Then you should try to assess the odds against such an occurrence happening (see Judging Coincidences, page 91). You should also check the possibility of cryptomnesia – that the witness may have unconsciously had prior knowledge of an event and so was 'steered towards it'.

It is also important to ask witnesses if they have experienced coincidences before. While everyone may be entitled to one or two extraordinary coincidences in their lifetime, if it happens regularly there may be something interesting happening. Take, for instance, the case of John Spencer, a prominent paranormal researcher and author who has been subject to an amazing number of coincidences in his private life.

In the early 1980s, John, as treasurer, organized the annual raffle of an association that he belonged to at a society lecture. In order to get the raffle moving he purchased five raffle tickets selecting them at random throughout the book. Around 500 tickets were sold before the lecturer was invited to draw the winning tickets from a drum that had been spun. The first ticket drawn out was John's. As organizer, he diplomatically declined first prize. The next ticket taken from the drum was also his. To hoots of derision from the gathering, he declined a prize for a second time. The third ticket produced a winner from the audience. However, the following ticket was again John's!

If this kind of thing happened once or twice it would be interesting. But John has notebooks full of such coincidences. It would be particularly rewarding if, as a researcher, you could find a subject who gets lots of coincidences as they may well be worth an in-depth study.

We then need to analyze why human beings could cause such effects. Persistent in many religions and philosophies is the idea of an original creator, who lays down laws by which we live, and many we may not yet comprehend. Maybe because of this link we can claim certain 'magical' powers though the channels of our unconscious minds.

To pursue this analogy further, if a deity created universal laws,

ANALYZING THE INFORMATION

• Coincidences may be more common than we suspect, but whether they are 'meaningful' depends upon the experience and belief system of the individual. Occasionally, they have the power to change our lives.

• Several categories of psi (including precognition, telepathy, causation, dreams and crisis apparitions) have been attributed to coincidence.

• We often need to be in an altered state of consciousness to observe coincidences. In such a mental mode could we also cause them?

• Chance itself may not be as random as we believe, having possibly a built-in bias towards coincidence.

• Consciousness has been linked with matter and probability at a fundamental level. Through our unconscious minds, can the need to achieve what we want actually make it happen? Library angels, poltergeists, the power prayer can all be examples of this.

it might be possible for the consciousness of 'mini-deities' to affect, change and alter such laws of time and space in their immediate vicinity, resulting in psychic powers, prophetic dreams, telepathy, and, of course, perhaps coincidences. In other words, at a local level, consciousness may change the odds or probability of an event taking place.

JUDGING COINCIDENCES

People unfamiliar with statistics often feel that events in their life are very rare coincidences when in fact they are not that uncommon. Take the following example: you travel to a town many miles away that you have never been to before and meet your next door neighbour in the High Street. You had no idea he was going to the town or that he had any connection with it. Is this a coincidence? Certainly, but not as rare as you might imagine. If you consider the total number of people going on journeys to distant towns in the whole country on one day, it could run into many thousands. If only a fraction of a percent of them meet people they know at the distant town, each will think it an amazing coincidence. And yet it may well happen several times each day over the whole country.

So the actual chance of someone meeting somebody they know in a distant town is not that unusual. To make this coincidence more unusual, there would need to be other factors involved which would increase the odds against it. Such factors might be the fact that this happened to one particular person on a regular basis or if both people involved were going to exactly the same building in the town, but for entirely unrelated reasons. Many coincidences are therefore not as amazing as their participants may think. However, when such coincidences happen repeatedly to one person, as in this case, there needs to be more explanation.

'Many coincidences are therefore not as amazing as their participants may think.'

DISCOVERING YOUR HIDDEN POWERS

'You might want to see if you have any psychic abilities yourself.'

EXTRA-SENSORY PERCEPTION (ESP) IS when a person can obtain information in some way other than through the normal senses of vision, hearing, touch, smell or taste. An example is telepathy, where someone can apparently read or receive another person's thoughts. Psychokinesis is the apparent ability of a person to influence their environment or objects physically without direct or indirect contact. This is commonly referred to as having the power of 'mind over matter'.

A person who could practise psychokinesis at will was Uri Geller, the famous Israeli psychic. Once, when guest of honour at the opening of a Fortean exhibition, he borrowed a key from another guest. The audience was very close to him, and the editors of this book were able to witness the event at close hand. In full view of everyone he proceeded to bend the key, apparently by gentle stroking alone.

• TESTING YOUR PSYCHIC ABILITIES •

While few of us are likely to get the chance to test the abilities of Uri Geller, you may still be approached by someone claiming psychic abilities. Or, indeed, you might want to see if you have any psychic abilities yourself, whether they have manifested themselves already or not. It is important to bear in mind that, whatever your own beliefs, most scientists do not believe in paranormal abilities.

Although there is some scientific evidence in favour of such abilities, it is not enough to persuade many scientists to change any of their theories quite yet. Therefore, if you investigate such apparent abilities you must do it in a scientifically convincing way. Anything less will be quickly dismissed and you may simply be wasting your time. Luckily, experiments to test paranormal abilities do not require special experience or vast amounts of expensive scientific equipment.

DIFFERENT PSYCHIC SKILLS

Many claimed psychic abilities, however bizarre they sound, are likely to amount to one of the phenomena listed in the table (right), or they could be a combination of them. For instance, someone who says they always know when a relative is about to call could be demonstrating either precognition or telepathy. It would depend on whether the relative thought about phoning at the moment our claimant sensed it. Precognition is dealt with in greater detail in Chapter 11, 'Premonitions'.

Remote viewing (the ability to obtain information about distant locations) is a particular technique discussed in detail in Chapter 6 (page 74). This, too, could be seen as one of two abilities: clairvoyance in directly viewing a distant scene or telepathy in sensing through the eyes of someone on the spot. Usually cases seem to involve several of these abilities in combination. It makes sense to treat them as general ESP.

Psychokinesis (PK) seems to work differently in that an influence is apparently travelling from a person instead of information arriving from outside. However, this ability may not be so isolated. Consider clairvoyance, for example. If someone wants to find out about an object or place, this might be achieved by 'sending' something out to probe them before returning with results. Indeed, in out-of-the-body experiences (OOBEs – see Chapter 9, page 102) this is exactly what the subject perceives.

In the telepathy example earlier, consider the phone call from the relative. In order to work, presumably some influence moves from the relative to the person they are about to phone. This influence will affect the brain of the person who then instinctively 'knows' they are about to be phoned.

It is obvious from this brief discussion that such labels as ESP, telepathy and PK are not necessarily clear cut. Indeed, it is conceivable they are all different facets of the same basic phenomenon. In the procedures that follow, it will not always be possible to distinguish between different phenomena. All one can say with certainty is that something is apparently happening that current science cannot readily explain.

> ‘ ... something is apparently happening that current science cannot readily explain.’

PSYCHIC DEFINITIONS

CLAIRAUDIENCE: apparent ability to hear spirit voices beyond the range of human hearing.

CLAIRVOYANCE: apparent ability to see not using the physical eyes.

EXTRA-SENSORY PERCEPTION (ESP): obtaining information in some way other than through the normal senses of vision, hearing, touch, smell or taste.

PRECOGNITION: the ability to foresee information about the future.

PSYCHOKINESIS (PK): the apparent ability of a person to influence or alter their environment physically without direct or indirect contact. This is commonly referred to as 'mind over matter'.

RETROCOGNITION: witnessing events from the past as if they were happening now.

TELEPATHY: the ability to read or receive another person's thoughts.

• INVESTIGATING A PSYCHIC EXPERIENCE •

The first thing to do when you hear that someone has had a psychic experience is to interview the claimant (see Chapter 1, 'Investigating' for more details). Get their basic details and then find out what history they have of any paranormal involvement:

◇ Did they, for instance, simply notice they were able to read thoughts or affect watches?

◇ Or were they deliberately setting out to develop such a gift through mediumistic or esoteric studies?

◇ Ask how much they knew about the paranormal before they started and how much they have learned since.

The next thing you need to do is to actually witness the claimed ability yourself. Do this in an informal situation in which the claimant feels comfortable. Certainly do not try to impose any restrictions on them. Allow the claimant to do whatever they want to and use whatever apparatus they might require. The idea is simply to try to witness the phenomena so that you can decide how to test it. The tests will obviously vary depending on what is claimed.

Next, see if it is possible to video or otherwise record events. Again, do not apply any restrictions or constraints, but note if the recording inhibits the phenomena at all (this is not unusual). This does not necessarily imply a hoax, but this aspect will be discussed later in this chapter.

'The idea is simply to try to witness the phenomena ...'

APPLYING 'CONTROLS'

Now start applying restrictions, or 'controls' as scientists call them. The idea is to eliminate any natural ways of producing the phenomena.

◇ Apply controls gradually so that more and more possible natural explanations are eliminated, and see if the phenomenon diminishes.

◇ There are some general ESP tests you might like to try after these initial experiments. It is not usually a good idea to do these first as they may put off your claimant, who might not see their relevance.

◇ Encourage the claimant at every stage and never give the impression that you are doubting their claim, as this may diminish their results.

• TESTING YOUR PSYCHIC POWERS •

There are some general tests that you can do to see if you have psychic abilities. They also illustrate the general principles you will need to apply to test more specific claimed abilities. So try these tests on yourself first in case you need to test someone else.

CARD GUESSING

Devised in the 1930s, Zener cards are often used to test for psychic abilities. They comprise five symbols (right): a star, a square, wavy lines, a cross and a circle. These cards are used instead of an ordinary deck because it is much easier to have just five variations to choose from. With the Zener card pack, out of 25 cards (five lots each of the five card types), someone will guess correctly five times. That is because at each guess you have one chance in five possibilities to get it right by luck.

◈ Decide the number of guesses (or trials) to be done and do not change it. The more trials you do, the more the overall score is likely to tend towards the average. You need to do as many trials as possible.

◈ Select a 'subject' (the one who guesses), a 'target' (the object whose value is being guessed, e.g. Zener cards), a 'sender' (who sees the target and 'sends' it to the subject) and an 'experimenter' (who oversees the test to make sure ordinary senses are not used).

◈ The experimenter shuffles the pack of cards and then hands them to the sender unseen.

◈ The sender then deals each card in such a way that he can see them but the subject cannot. For each card the subject will try to guess what it is.

◈ Make sure the subject cannot get the correct answer through normal sensory means. For example, the subject might see reflections in the sender's glasses or from a window behind. Ideally, position the subject in a different room.

◈ You may need more people – one to watch the subject, the other, the sender, to make sure that no sensory information passes between them: the room should be silent. Check for fraud such as a concealed radio or video device.

◇ Use a dice or computer to decide the order of the cards and lock them away in a safe. Then ask the subject to guess what each card is from the top of the deck. This helps impose more control.

◇ Also consider if your subject gets significantly fewer correct guesses than statistics suggest he should. Any deviation from chance, whether above or below is interesting scientifically. Whether it is 'good' or 'bad', 'positive' or 'negative' is simply a matter of our definition.

> *'It is also interesting to look for other patterns when interpreting the results.'*

INTERPRETING THE RESULTS

So what exactly are these experiments designed to measure? You might interpret it as telepathy (seeing the card through the eyes of the experimenter) or clairvoyance (seeing the card directly without need of another human). Either way, it is an example of ESP.

It is also interesting to look for other patterns when interpreting the results. It has often been noted that while the score for direct guessing is not significant, there may be a very good score for 'displacement'. Displacement means always looking at the card before or after the one that is supposed to be the target at the time of the trial. This could imply that the subject is in fact good at precognition or retrocognition.

You could, of course, arrange for the target to be determined well before or after the experiment so that you can look for time-shift effects. For example, the subject might imagine they are guessing cards that someone is looking at in another room, when in fact the targets have yet to be worked out! To make your results particularly impressive you could use 'double blind' methods. In such experiments, not only does the subject not know the target, neither does the experimenter.

The target may have been decided by an independent third party that

INTERESTING EFFECTS

• *One of the interesting results you may come across during your research is the 'experimenter effect'. This is where sceptical researchers tend to get worse results than those people inclined to believe in the paranormal.*

Another problem can be that initial good results often seem to tail off over time. Perhaps card guessing becomes a bit boring after a while. Attempts have been made to make ESP experiments more interesting and more like the field reports that inspired them, so instead of card guessing you might decide to try pictures instead.

For instance, you could use a pool of five photographs never seen by the subject. These should be as different from each other as possible. Get your sender to concentrate on each in turn and ask the subject to try to draw what he thinks it is. Then get a third party to judge which picture best matches the subject's attempts.

neither the experimenter nor subject has met. The results could be judged by yet another independent party. With this method there is no possible way that the experimenter could give clues to the subject, even if he wanted to. Such high standards are regularly used in laboratory experiments.

ANALYZING THE RESULTS

Once you have completed your card-guessing experiments, you need to find out if they are scientifically significant, and this can be done through statistics. There are many methods you could use, but they are beyond the scope of this book. Below is a simple method ('normal distribution' to statisticians) that anyone can follow and it will give some useful answers. It is applicable to card-guessing experiments and should really only be used with 100 trials or more. If you are getting apparently significant scores according to this method it would be useful to get your results checked by a statistician or paranormal research society.

First you need to get certain numbers from your results. These are as follows.

◇ The odds of being correct by chance (for example, if there are five variants in a pack of Zener cards the odds are 1/5 or 0.2).

◇ The total number of trials.

◇ The actual score: the number of targets you got right, for example, 28.

◇ The average score by chance: for example with 100 trials it is 100 x 0.2 (the odds) = 20.

Now you need to apply the following method:

◇ Get the result of '1 – odds of being correct', using 0.2 would be 1 – 0.2 = 0.8.

◇ Multiply this result by the odds of being correct, so here it would be 0.2 x 0.8 = 0.16.

◇ Multiply this result by the number of trials, say 100 for example, so here it would be 100 x 0.16 = 16.

◇ Now take the square root of the result (use a calculator), so in our example, the square root of 16 = 4.

◇ Now take the average score by chance from the actual score and divide it by the result of the previous step, for example, if we had an actual score of 28 then: 28 – 20 = 8 then divide by 4 = 2.

So, what does this final result (called the 'critical ratio' by statisticians) actually mean? Broadly speaking up to 1.96 results are considered not significant. Above 2.58 they are considered significant, with results between the two figures being a borderline case. Above 3.30 results would be considered highly significant. So our example of 2 might just be significant. If we had a score of 31 instead of 28, the result would have been 2.75 which would indeed have been statistically significant. Statisticians consider something to be 'significant' if there is a 1 in 100 chance, or less, of the result being caused by pure chance. In this case the critical ratio 2.58 indicates odds of 1 in 100.

• TABLE-TILTING •

If you used dice for testing yourself in the card guessing, did it occur to you that instead of 'reading' them to get the right result you might have actually been nudging them to the face you wanted? If you have these abilities you could try to levitate a table. It is possible for ordinary people to develop such a 'gift' through a technique known as a 'sitter group' or 'table-tilting'.

A SITTER GROUP

'The table may also slide about on the floor.'

In a sitter group several people sit around a small table, in a darkened room, with their hands on the top. After a while the table will often produce small sounds and movements. Over a number of regular sessions, these phenomena usually grow in magnitude and variety until they may resemble ones associated with physical mediumship. Physical mediums, much rarer nowadays than they used to be, have poltergeist-type effects occurring during their séances.

A whole variety of physical effects has been witnessed with this method and different ones may yet occur in the future. The range of effects is often slightly different from group to group, especially in the later stages of development and may depend on the exact make-up and circumstances of the group.

There have even been reported incidents where a table has moved or levitated while nobody was touching it at all. This is often only realized during group discussion after the event (remember that the sessions are usually in the dark). There have also been some even more dramatic effects recorded, such as the alleged appearance of physical objects which were not in the room to start with. In addition, some people have used sitter groups as a method of attempting to contact discarnate entities. There remains great scope for further study of these effects.

THE SITTER GROUP'S TECHNIQUES

Groups vary in how they operate, but the following points are derived mainly from the work of Ken

TABLE TILTING EFFECTS	
EARLY STAGES	Creaks and groans
	Slight movement
	Cold breezes
	Small lights
LATER STAGES	Rocking movement
	Sliding, lifting legs
	Complete levitation
	Appearance of objects

Batchelor, a psychologist and paranormal researcher who did much to develop the technique in a scientific manner.

❖ WHO IS INVOLVED?

The table-tilting, or sitter, group usually numbers around four persons. The attitude and personality of the people involved can be crucial to the success of the enterprise. The participants should, ideally, be open-minded about the research, and not hold any strong preconceptions about it. It is best if the participants are fellow researchers who want to gain some scientific knowledge, rather than sensation seekers.

'It is better not to draw too much attention to each event ...'

❖ WHERE ARE THEY HELD?

The group normally meets at the same location for each session. It is important to avoid interruption, so a private house is often used. Ideally, no one else should be in the house at the same time.

❖ WHEN DO THEY MEET?

The group normally meets regularly and fairly frequently, often weekly. It is important that the same people meet up. Make it clear at the outset that regular attendance is expected.

❖ HOW DOES IT WORK?

The table is generally on the small side. It should be light enough for one person to tilt it on their own when deliberately trying to do so. It should also be large enough to allow all the participants to put both of their hands on the top at once, without touching. The group members should be seated at the table in comfortable seats.

CREATING THE RIGHT ATMOSPHERE

A light-hearted atmosphere seems to be best during sittings. There is no need for meditation or chanting (which might even deter the phenomena). In early sessions particularly, most phenomena seem to take place when people are talking and not paying much attention to the table.

It is better not to draw too much attention to each event, but simply to accept it as a normal and natural part of the experiment. Attempts to record or control the phenomena, early on, usually reduce their incidence. It is thought that natural or accidental movements of the table that happen initially, may induce a belief in their psychokinetic origins. This thought may actually encourage the real PK in later sessions. Recording these phenomena, and possibly tracing them to their normal origins, destroys this apparently important ambiguity.

A TABLE-TILTING EXPERIENCE

Alan Cleaver, a paranormal researcher was involved with a group of researchers several years ago in a series of table-tilting experiments at a flat in north London. He recalls that four or five people sat around a small four-legged table in a dimly lit room with their hands resting on the table, not necessarily touching, and various methods were then used to evoke a response from the table.

Initially, much verbal encouragement was given by one of the group telling the other members to imagine one table leg or another rising off the floor. However, one of the best methods of getting a 'response' from the table was to ask: 'Is there anyone there?' The table would invariably lift up one leg and tap on the floor once for yes. Whether the group was addressing the spirit of a deceased person, a purely imaginary figure, or the table itself did not seem to matter. What seemed crucial was that they had something to blame for the movement of the table other than their own minds.

It was not too long before the table counted up to ten by tapping with its feet. Then it would lift up two legs, then three – but sadly never all four. It even became possible for the table to 'walk' around the room by standing up on two legs and then walking forward. On more than one occasion the table even walked up the walls. The members of the group always felt the movement was due almost entirely to the power of the mind in some way, but the exact mechanism eluded the researchers.

However, Alan remembers there were occasions when the table gave what the researchers termed 'sudden unexpected responses'. These were movements that caught the researchers by surprise and seemed not be produced by the 'group mind' but were highly suggestive of some outside influence. It was a tantalizing glimpse into precisely the phenomena reported in séance rooms. Sadly, it was never sustained enough for proper investigation.

'On one occasion a person who was highly sceptical of table-tilting came to one of the sessions. While she was in the room no phenomena were experienced. Indeed, members of the group felt there was the equivalent of a concrete block sitting on the table, holding it down. As one researcher commented, "Even a fork-lift truck could not lift this table". However, when the visitor left the room briefly, the table quickly burst into life and danced around the room. The moment the visitor came back, it dropped down to the floor, refusing to move once more.

It does seem to be possible to use a tape recorder, almost from the first session, as this does not seem to have too serious an effect on the phenomena. It is a useful way of recording the sequence of events and getting descriptions of them from what was said between the participants.

It is usual, and very wise, to write an account of the session once it is over. A tape recorder comes in very useful here. Such an account need not be detailed, but should give an idea of the type, frequency and strength of phenomena experienced. A subjective assessment of the mood of the participants on the night is also helpful.

VARYING FACTORS

- Use a different table.

- Sit in a different room.

- Choose a different venue.

- Change the layout of the room significantly, for example, rearranging the large pieces of furniture (but not the table itself).

- Play music in the background during a session.

- Possibly introduce guests sometimes, providing they are well briefed beforehand about what to expect.

SITTER GROUP EXPERIMENTS

Once regular, sustainable physical phenomena have been achieved, you could try changing various factors (see 'Varying Factors', left) to see if different effects can be created. The phenomena may well continue to evolve by themselves, without any conscious effort by the sitters. If so, an exact history of this process would be very interesting, particularly if it could be recorded in some way, such as with an infrared video camera. However, this can lessen the appearance of the phenomena. Some things, such as the moods of the group's members, will be different each time and should always be recorded, but other factors can be varied. For example, you should only change one factor at a time, and then persist with it for several sessions. Record any changes to the magnitude, character and variety of the phenomena with each change. There are many other useful experiments which could be tried out with sitter groups; the ideas here are merely suggestions.

In Ken Batchelor's group a video was made of a table-tilting with one of his group sitting on it. It was not possible to get full levitation on video even though it happened at other times. Interestingly, levitation would stop whenever the camera was switched on. This happened even though the camera was switched on without anyone else in the group knowing.

TRAVEL OUT
OF THE BODY

THERE ARE TWO PHENOMENA that are reported regularly that both suggest to those experiencing them that the human personality is trapped inside our physical body. The repercussions of such an observation, if verified, would obviously have enormous consequences for science, philosophy and religion. These phenomena are 'Out-of-the-body experiences' (OOBEs) and 'Near-death experiences' (NDEs). In the first, the person sees their own body as if from the outside. In the second the person, who is usually clinically dead (but who is later revived), experiences a journey away from their body, typically along a long tunnel.

Some people claim to be able to induce OOBEs at will and to be able to travel anywhere in the world, and even to other planets. Others tell of journeys to alternate planes inhabited by strange beings and the souls of the dead. The OOBE is taken by some to be evidence that the centre of human consciousness (i.e. the 'soul') lies outside the physical body, while most psychologists feel that the experience is simply an altered state of consciousness.

'Some people claim to be able to induce OOBEs at will ...'

• WHEN DID OOBES FIRST OCCUR? •

Because it has religious implications, the OOBE has a long recorded history. There are possible references to it in the Old Testament and the ancient Jewish *Pseudepigrapha*. St Paul is thought to have referred to it in his second letter to the Corinthians (12: 2-4). From the Middle Ages there are several accounts of the devoutly religious who were able to visit foreign lands while in a trance. Maria de Jesus, for example, was claimed to have converted a tribe of Mexican Indians in a series of OOBEs that she took from her Spanish convent. In addition to the Christian church, a great many other world religions have traditions of

102

OOBEs, including some shamanistic practices which deliberately induce the experiences through using hallucinogenic drugs.

The OOBE, in the form that it is most commonly encountered today, was first recorded in detail in the late 19th century. The Society for Psychical Research published recognizable accounts in its weighty 1886 tome, *Phantasms of the Living*, and Madame Blavatsky, founder of the spiritualistic religion of Theosophy, between 1877–1891 was the first to promote the concept of 'astral travel' beyond the body. A number of spiritualist mediums in the 1890s also claimed to be able to 'project their minds' to foreign locations, including a select number who said they travelled to Mars to meet with Martians.

The OOBE came more to the fore when a British psychical researcher, Hereward Carrington, met Sylvan Muldoon, an American who claimed to be able to have OOBEs at will. The two teamed up and in 1929 wrote *The Projection of the Astral Body*, an international bestseller that brought the phenomenon of the OOBE to the attention of the world at large.

Since this time the OOBE has been studied extensively by occultists and parapsychologists alike. A number of consistent 'astral travellers' have written up their experiences into books including, most famously, the American businessman Robert Monroe who discovered differing 'astral planes' and even claimed to have had sexual relations with the astral beings he encountered. His book, *Journeys Out-of-the-Body*, became an international bestseller.

Aside from these more famous astral travellers, the OOBE also commonly occurs as a spontaneous experience to individual people who have had no previous interest in occultist matters. These experiences, while being less dramatic than claimed trips to other planets and astral planes, are broadly consistent with each other and suggest that the OOBE, whatever its cause, is a definable experience. The paranormal investigator is more liable to encounter the spontaneous OOBE than those rare individuals that can induce OOBEs at will.

'... the OOBE also commonly occurs as a spontaneous experience ...'

• WHAT IS AN OOBE? •

Most OOBEs are linked to the relaxation of the body and to sleep, but there are a number of different mental states in which OOBEs have been reported to occur. The OOBE is a common part of the near-death experience (see page 109) and has also been associated with illness, particularly high fevers, life-threatening accidents and anaesthetics.

Alternatively, OOBEs have also been known to be induced by ritualistic dancing or rhythmic drumming or by the taking of relaxant or hallucinogenic drugs. There are a number of techniques said to be able to induce an OOBE, most of which are based on relaxation methods followed by an attempt to shift the centre of consciousness from the physical to the astral body (see 'Inducing an OOBE', page 108). Some techniques rely on tricking or forcing the astral body away from the physical body.

Whether spontaneous or induced, the vast majority of OOBEs involve a person who will almost always have been lying or sitting down and have been in the process of falling asleep or waking up. Although OOBEs have happened to those who are awake and animated (see below), these are exceedingly rare indeed.

In the case of a spontaneous OOBE, the person will commonly not be aware of leaving their body and will suddenly awake to find themselves in an out-of-the-body state. Those who do remember the process of 'leaving' their bodies are normally in the process of waking up or falling asleep at the time and therefore in a semi-conscious state. During the 'leaving-the-body' process there are common reports of people hearing unusual noises (commonly a low buzzing sound), of being paralyzed or feeling strange 'vibrations' within the body. Many of these descriptions bear a resemblance to the disorder known as 'sleep paralysis' (see 'The Psychological Explanation', page 116).

ASTRAL TRAVELLING

• *Descriptions from 'astral travellers' are one of the most controversial aspects of OOBEs. Although most people who have had OOBEs believe that their experience took place in the 'real world', there are often significant differences in the descriptions of locations given by astral travellers and those in reality.*

Sometimes these differences are severe. In the 1890s the medium Hélène Smith described the planet Mars as having an equable climate, canals, bridges and a civilization of human-like beings, something that the modern space age has disproved. Other differences are small and include clothing, the colours of objects and details of conversation. Such differences, both big and small, are explained by occultists as being due to subtle interactions between the astral and physical planes. Alternatively, psychologists cite these differences as evidence that the astral world is a creation of the mind.

INITIAL FEELINGS

In the initial out-of-the-body phase the person will often suddenly find themselves conscious and floating a couple of metres above their own body. The clichéd phrase, 'I awoke to find myself floating near the ceiling and looking down on my body in bed' is often used. Other 'leaving' experiences include people awakening to find themselves standing at the end of their bed, looking at their bodies. In the case of drug induced OOBEs, people sometimes report that their consciousness simply expands beyond the physical limits of their body until the OOBE state is achieved.

The so-called astral body, a transparent version of the physical body, is rarely reported in spontaneous OOBE cases, perhaps because these experiences tend to be short-lived and confused. Regular astral travellers often report the presence of an astral body and that it is capable of being seen by the living under the right conditions. The famous 'silver cord', which is said to connect the astral body to the physical body and which, if broken, will lead to death, is rarely reported. It would seem that the silver cord, the idea of which was suggested by Madame Blavatsky in 1875, is a part of OOBE folklore and is generally only seen by those who had some prior knowledge of it before their experience.

• FLOATING
Many people who have experienced OOBEs, describe the feeling of floating above their body.

This sensation of being out of the body is apparently vivid and realistic and quite distinctive from the fuzzy sensation of dreaming. Many spontaneous OOBEs are very frightening to their participants and the experience is generally short-lived, with most of the individual's focus being on trying to get back into their body. In such cases details are liable to be scant, the witness often having been too frightened to take in any real detail from what is a brief experience that occurs almost exclusively in just one room. Those who repeatedly have OOBEs, or who are not frightened by them, can often travel great distances and report details of other rooms in the house or outside landscapes and locations.

• OOBE EXPERIMENTS •

'Those who repeatedly have OOBEs ... can often travel great distances ...'

In contrast to this are experiments where an OOBE is said to provide apparently unknowable information, implying that the phenomenon really does involve the mind's leaving the body. The most famous of these were done in the 1960s by the American parapsychologist Charles Tart who studied those who were able to induce OOBEs at will.

In a laboratory, Tart placed a piece of paper containing a random set of five numbers on an out-of-reach shelf above a bed. The person was then asked to try to read the number on the high shelf by lying on the bed and having an OOBE. Tart had a great deal of success with one person in particular, called Miss Z., who correctly gave him the number. A similar experiment between parapsychologist Karlis Osis and Ingo Swann produced a number of successes, but that time drawings were used instead of numbers. In some apparently OOBE-related experiments described in *Phantasms of the Living*, people managed not only to project themselves into the bedrooms of others, but their astral bodies were also sometimes witnessed by the poor unfortunates that they chose to visit.

Perhaps the most controversial aspect of OOBEs is the astral planes that are said to exist at different levels of 'psychic vibration' to our own and that can be visited while in the astral body. This concept derives much from Eastern philosophy and was, like the silver cord, originally promoted in the late 19th century by Madame Blavatsky and the Theosophists. Seasoned astral travellers claim that there are several different astral planes to which the astral body has access. These planes are alternative realities where a whole range of differing experiences can be had, including meeting with the souls of the dead and other astral beings or even travelling to parallel universes. The paranormal investigator is, in all likelihood, unlikely to encounter people who have journeyed to other astral planes and those interested in this more exotic side to the OOBE should consult the books by Robert Monroe.

'The ending of an OOBE is often as sudden as its beginning.'

THE END OF AN OOBE

The ending of an OOBE is often as sudden as its beginning. In spontaneous cases the person will commonly end what has been a scary ordeal by 'willing' themselves back into their body (sometimes through prayer) or by relaxing. The arrival back in the physical body is sometimes described as being so swift that the physical body jerks. Accustomed astral travellers often just 'think themselves back into their bodies'.

There would appear to be no real physical after-affects associated with the OOBE. Some people often interpret their OOBE in religious terms and use it as evidence of an afterlife or of the body having a soul. Others look on it as a paranormal experience for which they have no explanation.

• INVESTIGATING AN OOBE EXPERIENCE •

OOBEs are a relatively common paranormal experience, and various surveys estimate that between 8 and 15 per cent of the population have had one and that there is no bias toward age, sex or social background. They do, however, tend to be isolated in their occurrence and although such cases are easy to find, several years can often have elapsed before the paranormal investigator arrives on the scene. Getting a 'fresh' case is a tricky business and, because of the spontaneous nature of the phenomenon, a matter of luck as much as anything else.

THE OOBE

The following two short accounts illustrate two types of OOBE. The first, from a woman interviewed by the author in 1998, who had recurrent OOBEs during her teenage years – her experience is likely to be a case of sleep paralysis (see 'The Psychological Explanations', page 112). The second case is an OOBE that occurred in 1970 to a 20-year-old florist that has certain similarities to the NDE.

'I woke up, possibly already in a panic, and couldn't move any part of my body, it felt as though I was stuck to the bed. I then felt unable to breath properly. My immediate thought was that something was seriously wrong. I thought I should shout for help, but I couldn't (it wasn't that no sound was coming out – I just couldn't move my mouth at all). I remember thinking that I must be having some sort of brain haemorrhage or seizure and that I was about to die.

As I got more and more scared, I started to have what I suppose was an intense panic attack. I was trying to shout and breath and sit up all at the same time. I also felt like I was exerting a lot of pressure on my brain. I then began to float out of my body – I felt myself float towards the ceiling and look down at myself, not that I turned and looked down, like I could see all around

somehow – I felt like I was looking at the situation from an external point of view. In this state I had a feeling of space and felt numb (almost calm) to the feelings of panic that I was aware I was really experiencing. All of a sudden I was able to move, my arms jerked and I sat up right, eventually the panic subsided and I went back to sleep. I didn't tell anyone about this experience.'

I had been lying on the sofa for a few hours... I was completely relaxed and felt as if I were drifting off to sleep. Then I felt a weight pressing on my face and suddenly I was aware that... I had actually risen up to ceiling height. I turned over and seemed to hover... I could see everything in the room quite clearly, even myself lying on the sofa... Then I saw what I can only describe as a coloured door floating in front of me. A voice with-in me seemed to say, "Open the door to seek knowledge." And as I moved toward it the door swung open to reveal a different coloured door... [I had] the feeling that... if I did not return to my body I would have to move on... I was told it was not time for me to go, I must return for a while longer as there was something else I had to do.'

(Extract from The Unexplained, Vol. 1, p.145)

'The mystery of death holds a fear and fascination to every human being ...'

To find OOBE cases, the best method is simply to mention your interest to friends and relatives – somebody is bound to know of one. If this does not work, simply advertise for cases in local newspapers, paranormal magazines, notice boards (universities are the best place for this – but get permission first) or on the Internet. Paranormal organizations may occasionally get cases and it is worth joining and signalling an interest to them.

The other means of investigating OOBEs is to try to induce one yourself. There are a number of methods for doing this and a commonly used one, the Christos technique, is described here.

INDUCING AN OOBE

There are several means of inducing an OOBE, most of which involve what might be loosely termed relaxation, self-hypnosis or meditation techniques. One of the more successful of these is the 'Christos technique'. This method was developed by an Australian journalist named G. Glaskin in 1974 and involves trying to displace your centre of consciousness from your physical body. You will, ideally, need two friends to help you out.

◈ Take your shoes off and lie down on your back in a slightly darkened room and get comfortable.

◈ Play some gentle music in the background.

◈ Next, get a helper to massage your feet and ankles. They will need to do this very firmly indeed to get the full effect.

◈ The second person should also massage your forehead by placing the soft part of their clenched fist on it and rubbing hard. This needs to continue for several minutes.

After some time you will begin to feel slightly light-headed and even a bit disorientated. Your feet should start to tingle as well. If you are trying this alone, then the alternative is to use standard relaxation techniques:

◈ Try breathing in and out slowly and deeply while imagining that there is a warm relaxing sensation that starts at your feet and then moves up through your body.

◈ As this warm feeling passes up through your body, mentally describe the effect it is having on each part of it. By the time the feeling has reached your head your body will feel totally relaxed and incapacitated.

When you are completely relaxed, start imagining that your head and feet are stretching slightly and then returning to their normal shape. Keep doing this, imagining that both your head and feet are stretching further each time you do it. When you can imagine them stretching your body length by another metre or so, start to imagine that your body is swelling up outwards until it fills the entire room. This may sound weird, but the feeling that you are indeed filling the entire room can be very realistic.

One of your helpers (in their absence, you will have to do this yourself) should then ask you to imagine that you are outside your front door and to ask you to describe everything you can see there. They should ask you to float up into the air so that you have a reasonable view of your town or village. It is from this point that the distinction between being inside and outside the body may become blurred.

To focus your mind and enhance the experience, your companions must get you to describe everything that you can see in as much detail as possible. Fly over the landscape, and give a vivid description of everything you see.

The session will normally end spontaneously with the subject simply waking up but you can be talked back down to earth if need be (if you have helpers). A reported side-effect of this technique is that some people do not find themselves in their astral bodies but instead wake up in what has been interpreted as a past life.

INTERVIEW CHECKLIST

When interviewing somebody about their OOBE follow the general interviewing techniques outlined in Chapter 1, 'Investigating'. Concentrate on gathering details about not only the experience itself, but about the lead-up to it and the mental state of the person at the time it occurred (were they under stress or perhaps recently bereaved, for example). If possible, ask to see where the experience occurred and photograph/sketch the location it to get a better idea of any descriptions you are given.

The ultimate goal is to try and find some form of evidence that the OOBE was a real (as opposed to imagined) experience. To do this you will need to have proof that the person saw or heard something during their OOBE that they could not otherwise have known. This proof may need to be verified by others, in which case politely ask for names and phone numbers of other witnesses and get permission to contact them. If permission is refused then accept it: the art of paranormal investigation has a bad enough reputation as it is without adding harassment to it!

'Near-death experiences have a considerable track record in history.'

• THE NEAR-DEATH EXPERIENCE •

The mystery of death holds a fear and fascination to every human being, and the speculation about what happens to our mind, and its collection of memories and experiences, underpins the religious doctrine of every human culture. Death may not, however, be the one-way trip that it may appear, and there is a very good tradition of people who, having been revived from a medically dead state, who have reported glimpses of a strange and wonderful world that seems to offer first-hand evidence that an afterlife does exist. This phenomenon is known as the near-neath experience or NDE.

THE HISTORY OF NDES

Near-death experiences have a considerable track record in history. The earliest recorded one is thought to be in Plato's book, *The Republic*, which relates how a Greek soldier was returned to life with tales of an afterlife where, after judgement, the soul could take passageways to either heaven or hell.

The first proper writings about people's experience during death come with the advent of popular Christianity from the 5th century onward. Pope Gregory the Great (540–604 AD) recorded three examples of NDE and during the Middle Ages there were a great many tales of people having died and visited either a heavenly paradise or a fiery hell.

The modern era in the study of NDE began in 1892 when Heim published *The Experience of Dying from Falls*, in which he collected together the experiences of mountaineers who had had serious falls and been close to death. Heim concluded that, rather than being scared and in pain, the injured and dying climbers had experienced feelings of calm and peace. They had, said Heim, '... fallen into heaven'.

• WHAT IS AN NDE? •

The NDE has been widely studied by both amateurs and professionals and has a much more structured series of stages than the OOBE. The subject has had countless books and articles written on it and there is even an academic *Journal of Near-Death Studies*. Raymond Moody, the discoverer of the NDE, provides a composite account of an NDE in *Life After Life* which illustrates all its main points:

'A man is dying and, as he reaches the point of greatest physical distress, he hears himself pronounced dead by his doctor. He begins to hear an uncomfortable noise, a loud ringing or buzzing, and at the same time feels himself starting to move through a long dark tunnel. Once through the tunnel he finds himself outside his own physical body, but

NEAR-DEATH EXPERIENCE – THE REALITY

The NDE was actually only popularized in 1975 when Raymond Moody published his international best-seller *Life after Life*. In this classic work Moody, a clinical psychiatrist from Georgia, presents extracts from cases involving more than one hundred people who, having been pronounced dead, were revived only to tell tales of a journey into an afterlife. These stories, despite coming from people who had never met, were remarkably consistent and seemed to suggest that there was a common experience that humans undergo after death.

Life after Life, was greeted with enthusiasm by the public and scepticism by the scientific community. Unknown to Moody, two other psychiatrists, Russell Noyes and Elisabeth Kubler-Ross, had separately been conducting their own research into NDE. Their results were identical to those of Moody's, adding weight to the theory that NDE is a common phenomemon

Other scientists were openly critical of Moody's NDE work. One of these, the cardiologist Michael Sabom, denounced *Life after Life* as being a work of fiction and set about interviewing patients that he had revived from near-fatal heart attacks. He was shocked to find that not only did his patients commonly report NDEs, but also they were exactly as Moody had described. Sabom became converted and went on to conduct his own extensive research into NDEs.

In the following decades, study after study has confirmed that this phenomenon is real. Although many in the scientific community still argue about what it actually represents, the NDE is now an accepted fact.

Below is the testimony from 'R', a 78-year-old man whose heart stopped during a stay in hospital in May 1997. His heart was started again using several electric shocks. It took him over 24 hours to remember his experience, although the nurses were apparently aware that he had undergone an unusual experience during his revival.

May 1997

'I was rushed to the General Hospital and admitted to the I.C.U. with heart problems... I lay on what seemed to be a bed, when suddenly I jumped up with arms outstretched and shouted. Somebody or something guided me towards a very big multi-coloured star.
I could hear faint singing coming from the star. The singing grew louder as I drew nearer. I approached the star with outstretched hands. I could see what appeared to be thousands of people, arms outstretched, and shouting "Millennium". I was about to enter [the star] when a voice above me called "Go Back. Revive my teaching by uniting the world's religions." At that precise moment I felt I was being taken from the star. Farther away from the star I distinctly saw three people clutching me and pulling me back to Earth... The nurses [later] explained that they were the three people who pulled me back [NOTE: it was three nurses who revived R.]... I laughed and said I was in orbit.'

111

'Others feel themselves being 'pulled' back towards their physical body...'

still in the intermediate physical environment, and he sees his own body from a distance, as though he were a spectator. He watches the attempts to resuscitate him from this unusual vantage point and is in a state of emotional upheaval.

'After a while he collects himself and becomes more accustomed to his odd condition. He notices that he still has a "body", but one of a very different nature and with very different powers from the physical body he has left behind. Soon other things begin to happen. Others come to meet and to help him. He glimpses the spirits of relatives and friends who have already died, and a loving, warm spirit of a kind he has never encountered before – a being of light – appears before him.

'This being mentally asks him a question, to make him evaluate his life and helps him along by showing him a panoramic, instantaneous playback of the major events of his life. At some point he finds himself approaching some sort of barrier or border, apparently representing the limit between earthly life and the next life. Yet, he finds that something is holding him back and he must go back to earth, that the time for his death has not yet come. At this point he resists, for by now he is taken up with his experiences in the afterlife and does not want to return. He is overwhelmed by intense feelings of joy, love and peace. Despite his attitude, though, he somehow reunites with his physical body and recovers.

'Later he tries to tell other people but he has trouble doing so. In the first place, he can find no human words adequate to describe these unearthly episodes. He also finds that others scoff at what has happened, so he stops telling other people. Still, the experience affects his life profoundly, especially his views about death and its relationship to life.' (Extract from Moody, 1975, p.21-23)

Moody's description of an NDE is still the accepted model and it is in this form that the paranormal investigator is likely to encounter the NDE. Moody initially listed 15 key stages in the NDE but this list has, over the years, been generally whittled down to five. The investigator will need to be aware of these five key stages when listening to an account of somebody's brush with death. After physical death, the order of occurrence of these stages are:

◇ A feeling of calm and inner peace.

◇ The separation of the 'spiritual body' from the physical body, normally in the form of an out-of-the-body experience.

◇ The spiritual body then enters a realm of darkness, commonly described as being like a tunnel.

◇ There will then be a bright light, often at the end of the tunnel.

◇ The spiritual body will then enter this light (or be stopped from entering it by a being/beings) and be in the 'afterlife'.

These five stages form what has been termed 'the core near-death experience'. Surveys show that the number of people experiencing each stage decreases dramatically down the list with, according to Kenneth Ring, 60 per cent of near-death experiencers having stage 1; 37 per cent stage 2; 23 per cent stage 3; 16 per cent stage 4; and only 10 per cent stage 5. Based on this, the investigator is statistically more likely to encounter people who have had only the first couple stages of a NDE, with the classically described dark tunnel actually being a much rarer experience.

Around this core experience the investigator may also hear other common stories associated with the journey into the light. During the out-of-the-body experience in stage 2, people commonly find themselves looking from a vantage point that is above and to one side of their own body. For example, if in an operating theatre, they will often be looking at the proceedings from a ceiling corner.

On the return to the body and following questioning, the person may be able to give details of the scene surrounding their body during the OOBE, including details of people's actions, clothing and conversations and of near-by scenery or machinery. These descriptions are frequently verified by witnesses and are strong evidence that, despite being clinically dead, the person was somehow able to see or sense events around them.

 RETURNING TO THE BODY

• *The return to the body can also vary. Many people simply wake up in hospital, or wherever, with no memory of their return journey. Others feel themselves being 'pulled' back towards their physical body while in the OOBE or dark tunnel stage. Others are given the option to return by spiritual people that they may meet, while others are told to return, often against their will. Some people even report being given a 'push' back down the dark tunnel by a being who resides in the light. People commonly report being told that 'their time has not yet arrived' or that they are 'too early'.*

During this state they may also report hearing rhythmic noises or even calming 'celestial music' that may continue to accom-pany them as they enter the next stage, which is the darkness or dark tunnel.

GOING DOWN THE TUNNEL

Just before, or during, the journey in the dark tunnel, the person may meet with dead relatives or some form of supernatural being that will guide them toward the bright light. They may also undergo a review

'There are no social taboos about having been revived from death ...'

of their lives which particularly focuses on major events or decisions that may have changed the direction of that individual's path. Some people see this review as being a religious judgement of their actions before they are allowed into the afterlife.

At the light itself, those that have not been accompanied along the tunnel may then be confronted by their relatives or a recognizable supernatural being. These people may converse with the person or, in the case of relatives, have an emotional reunion. The place that the person may find themselves in beyond the light varies enormously. Some people report being in a fantastic garden, others that it is just a place of light and love. Others report more sinister experiences that would match the notion of hell as we know it.

• THE EFFECT OF AN NDE •

An NDE often has a profound effect on the individual. Many will become religious and there has been more than one atheist converted as a consequence. Some people experience such a feeling of love and tranquillity that they are angry that they have been returned to the Earth. A great many people lose any fear of death and some, including a relative of mine who was briefly re-united with her dead husband after a massive stroke, look forward to the day when they can return to the afterlife.

The style and type of NDE discussed above has been gathered almost exclusively by Americans and Europeans from people with Christian backgrounds. Other cultures, too, have their NDEs but the number of studies done on these is very limited indeed. The investigator must, however, be aware of any cultural bias that occurs within first-hand accounts that they may encounter.

• NDES ABROAD •

Surveys done in India and China have found that, while many basic elements of the five-stage 'core experience' remain similar, the beings that may greet the person and the world they encounter beyond the light are definitely culturally biased.

Christians will see Jesus, meet God and see dead relatives and will be happily taken to heaven (or occasionally hell). Hindus will be escorted by Hindu deities and will normally fight to be sent back to Earth, refusing to go into the light. Christians will commonly return because they are concerned about relatives or because 'their time has not yet come'. Chinese and Indians are normally sent back because they were summoned too early by mistake, sometimes because of an apparent clerical error by those collecting souls. Comparisons of modern NDEs with those from the Middle Ages have also found significant differences, the most noticeable of which is the much larger number of medieval people that reported visions of hell compared with today.

PLACING ADVERTISEMENTS

• *For more immediate cases you will have to place an advertisement in local news-papers or specialist magazines. In such an advert, do not be too specific about the kind of experience you wish to study, simply ask for accounts from people who have 'died' and come back to life. Alternatively, cases can be received through nurses, but there are problems here with both patient confidentiality and the ethics of interviewing somebody about death in a hospital ward.*

• INVESTIGATING A • NEAR-DEATH EXPERIENCE

Unlike an out-of-the-body experience, a near-death experience is not something that the investigator can induce, so you will be wholly reliant upon finding cases for yourself. This is not as tricky as it first sounds.

There are no social taboos about having been revived from death, and people who have had an NDE are often so enthusiastic that they will talk about it to anybody who wants to listen. So, by making it known that you are interested in such cases, you will often find that people will pass on the word and do much of the work for you. This can, however, take some time to work and you may end up with experiences that occurred to people several years ago and which, therefore, may have become embellished with time.

TACTFUL TECHNIQUES

Follow the general interview guidelines outlined in Chapter 1, but take care. NDEs are a very sensitive subject and a great deal of tact will be needed on the part of the investigator. Some people may be elderly or have undergone unpleasant experiences such as a car accident. Others may have strong religious convictions or will be upset at the thought of recalling meetings with relatives.

Regarding the experience itself, make sure that any accounts that are associated with OOBEs are as detailed as possible, as these may be verifiable later on by other witnesses, such as medical personnel. Details of conversations, specific clothing on witnesses and, in the case of NDEs, of any medical procedures that were seen to be carried out are particularly useful.

VERIFYING THE NDE

This can be more tricky, especially if it occurred a long time ago or in a distant location, but there are things you can do.

' ... make sure that any accounts that are associated with OOBEs are as detailed as possible ...'

'NDEs and OOBEs are also closely associated with lucid dreaming ...'

❖ If you are given names and addresses of witnesses then contact them, personally if possible.

❖ Do not reveal any details you have from the revived person himself and concentrate on collecting descriptions of the scene in the minutes before and after the temporary death of the individual, again concentrating on conversations, clothing and procedures.

❖ In the case of medical witnesses, make sure you ask whether the person concerned was technically dead for a while. This might seem obvious but in one survey of 58 near-death experiences, 30 were not actually in danger of dying, but merely thought that they were. Also ask if the person had volunteered their story without knowing that they had temporarily died or whether it was told after they had been told of their revival. If any medical evidence is available (which it rarely is) then ask if you can see it and/or photocopy or photograph it (this is even more doubtful).

SIMILAR SYMPTOMS

SLEEP PARALYSIS

The descriptions of paralysis, low humming noises, floating and bodily vibration experienced in OOBEs have a very close similarity to the phenomenon of sleep paralysis. In this condition the muscle paralysis that protects us from violent movements in our sleep does not get turned off upon waking and the person may find themselves paralysed for a few seconds or minutes after waking.

HYPNAPOMPIC HALLUCINATIONS

Sleep paralysis is often accompanied by hypnapompic hallucinations, a situation where our dreams intrude into our waking world, producing a variety of non-existent sensations, including the feeling of floating above the body.

The first experience described on page 107 is almost certainly a case of sleep paralysis with a combined hypnapompic hallucination.

OTHER

NDEs have been variously explained over the years as being caused by a lack of oxygen in the brain, chemical changes, a defence mechanism to take the fear out of death or evolutionary memories of the birth canal – none of these has much credibility. Recent research has found that controlled doses of the drug ketamine can produce identical symptoms to the NDE, suggesting that it may be a mind-centred experience.

The paranormal investigator should be aware of alternative explanations, particularly sleep paralysis, and is advised to have some knowledge of them before embarking on a case.

• THE PSYCHOLOGICAL EXPLANATION •

Despite initial scepticism, both the NDE and OOBE have been verified as genuine experiences by psychologists and have, consequently, been extensively studied. However, most of the resulting theories about what they are have little to do with the paranormal.

Several examinations of the psychological profiles of those who have had OOBEs and NDEs have shown that they are likely to:

◈ Have fantasy-prone personalities or an active imagination.

◈ To have a capacity for absorption (the ability to be so engrossed in a subject that the person blocks out all other sensory information, for example, being absorbed in a book).
   Both these conditions are associated with many other paranormal experiences including seeing apparitions, UFOs or lake monsters.

NDEs and OOBEs are also closely associated with lucid dreaming, a condition where somebody may suddenly find themselves awake inside their own dream landscape. Other researchers have associated both experiences with hysteria and schizophrenia and it has been noted that seizures in the temporal lobe region of the brain can produce very similar sensations.

CONTACT WITH
THE SPIRITS

MANY PEOPLE ARE QUITE happy not to have to think about what happens to them after they die, preferring to put off deciding whether they believe in an afterlife and whether your spirit lives on. But for some people the question of life after death is answered by their beliefs in spiritualism. In your role as an investigator and researcher you will need to consider what to say if you are asked for your opinion on an unusual incident that has happened to someone. You may be told by a recently bereaved woman how she regularly feels her late husband's presence or a person may talk to you about a visit to a medium and how it produced information on the 'afterlife' and messages from various deceased relatives. You need to know how to assess what is confided to you, and how to go about constructing your own research programme to find out more.

• STAYING NEUTRAL •

'You need to know how to assess what is confided to you ...'

A neutral stance is vital here, as it is essential to stop your own beliefs from intruding on your assessment of the incident. Many people have kept their beliefs about the afterlife more or less intact since childhood. Most religions do not encourage deep questioning or the consideration of alternative belief systems, so an event that goes against accepted religious teachings can come as a deep shock.

When the person is psychologically vulnerable, it is important not to attempt to replace their shaken beliefs with a religion or philosophy that you feel provides more answers. Keeping an open mind means acknowledging that you do not have all the answers and that the other person, or even a third party, may be right. A basic understanding of other religions' attitudes to death will help you to be sympathetic to the implications of the case you are involved in and should help you avoid suggestions that might give offence or be distressing.

SPIRITUAL TERMS

CONTROL: a spirit who 'controls' the medium, generally his or her guide, taking over the body of trance mediums.

CLAIRVOYANT: an ability to see not using the physical eyes (see also page 93).

CLAIRAUDIENT: an ability to hear not using the physical ears.

CLAIRSENTIENCE: a combination of clairaudience and clairvoyance.

ECTOPLASM: a substance produced by physical mediums and formed into bodies, or body parts, or 'rods' to manipulate such things as trumpets to amplify the communicator's voice.

MATERIALIZATION: the appearance of a spirit using a material such as ectoplasm to clothe the spiritual body. A materialization medium uses these effects.

MEDIUM: a general term for a person who is sensitive to vibrations from the spirit world and is able to convey messages between that world and this.

MENTAL MEDIUM: one who uses skills such as clairaudience, clairvoyance and clairsentience to produce messages from the departed.

PHYSICAL MEDIUM: one who produces physical effects such as materializations and transfiguration.

PSYCHIC ARTIST: a medium who produces drawings or sketches of communicators seen clairvoyantly.

PSYCHIC DETECTIVE: a medium who helps or tries to help police with their work, mainly in tracing missing people or tracking down murderers and the bodies of their victims.

PSYCHOMETRIST: a medium or person who uses a physical object to help produce messages. For example, the medium holds a watch owned by a deceased person and uses this to tune in to the communicator.

SÉANCE: generally interchangeable with 'sitting'. Both imply a meeting, often private, where one or more spirits will transmit messages through a medium.

SPIRIT GUIDE: a spirit allocated to a living person and acting as a sort of guardian, often mentioned during sittings or drawn by psychic artists.

TRANCE MEDIUM: one whose personality is taken over by a control during a séance. The medium is generally unaware of what happens during the séance.

TRANSFIGURATION MEDIUM: a medium whose face and other physical features are seen to change to reflect the features of the spirit whose message they are currently communicating.

Researchers living in the western world will be dealing mainly with cases from a practising or nominally Christian population. Sincerely held religious beliefs will prevent some people from taking part in survival research. Many Christians find the idea of actively seeking contact with the next world deeply offensive or disturbing. Spiritualists, however, would counter with the statement that they are making themselves open to contact and cannot force the deceased to contact loved ones against their will.

For the sake of our research we need to assume that contact with the spirit world is indeed possible. You may decide after years of unconvincing evidence that this is not the case, but that will be a personal judgement.

'They may be able to read the sitter's mind.'

DEALING WITH BEREAVEMENT

Bereavement is a difficult time for anyone, giving rise to complex feelings of loss and guilt. Once the initial deep sense of grief has abated, the bereaved person may find that the questions outnumber the officially sanctioned answers. Maybe a loved one has died in a manner felt to be unfair, or a person has a strong feeling of having been contacted by a deceased friend or relation. That is when many begin to seek evidence of life after death.

It must be pointed out in this connection that it is not the researcher's responsibility to act as a bereavement counsellor. There are bereavement organizations that exist to provide the necessary individual or group counselling. The researcher's task is to analyze the evidence that a person's spirit lives on in a detached, scientific manner.

• SURVIVAL OF BODILY DEATH •

Despite centuries of philosophical speculation, the matter of what part of the personality survives after death, if any, remains a moot point. The difference between the personality and the soul is not clear. Also nobody can say whether memories that are stored in the physical brain survive with the departed 'soul'.

You will also need to consider at what stage following death the deceased may be available for contact.

If we assume that after death the personality survives with its memory intact, you should analyze what interest the deceased has in making themselves available for contact.

We have all heard tales about spirits returning to help clear up some mystery, such as telling remaining family members where they hid the money box, or to point an accusing finger at an undiscovered murderer. One particular American case was regarded by the late researcher and author D. Scott Rogo as excellent evidence of survival (see 'The Chaffin Will Affair', page 125). However, many such cases are fictitious and are 'ghost stories' rather than evidence of an actual departed soul's purposeful return.

FINDING GOOD EVIDENCE

If a communication that is received from a deceased person through a medium could be proved to comprise information unavailable from any

THE CROSS-CORRESPONDENCES

Often put forward as a case that proves survival, partly because of the complexity of the evidence and partly because the impetus seemed to come from the deceased parties, this case is still in need of a full investigation over 90 years after the event.

The founders of the Society for Psychical Research, Frederic Myers, Henry Sidgwick and Edmund Gurney, had all died by the early 1900s. A number of the trance mediums working with their successors were intellectuals first and psychics second, but the messages they were about to receive went beyond their knowledge. The mediums included Margaret Verrall and her daughter Helen, the sister of Rudyard Kipling (Mrs Holland in the reports), and a 'Mrs Willett', later revealed to be the British stateswoman Winifred Coombe-Tenant. What brought the mediums together was a project seemingly instigated by the SPR's late leaders with the aim of proving survival.

The communications that they received largely took the form of messages jotted down by the psychics. Taken alone, the jottings meant nothing, but once the pieces from each psychic were put together the meaning became clear. Mrs Holland, who was living in India, began to receive automatic writing (see page 127) purporting to come from F. H. Myers. His material contained quotations from classical Greek and Latin works. On a visit to England in 1906 her scripts were linked with those of Leonore Piper, an American medium also visiting England at the time and producing obscure communications with classical references.

At one séance with Mrs Piper, the sitter, J. G. Piddington, received a message from Myers telling him he would find a clue in automatic writing produced through Mrs Verrall. In fact, the key to understanding how the messages slotted together was in a script written by Helen Verrall.

The messages went on until around 1910, each series taking a number of weeks to produce and put together. The papers have been preserved, but can only be fully appreciated with the type of classical scholarship that typified a certain class in the years before the First World War. Men such as F. H. Myers himself, in fact.

The late survival researcher, Robert Thouless, is quoted as having said that the cross-correspondences were 'a badly designed experiment' since the evidentiality is hard to judge. However, most of the people who examined the scripts at the time believed they were good evidence for survival. Only Frank Podmore, also of the SPR, claimed they could be accounted for by telepathy between the mediums, particularly since Mrs Verrall was the wife of a classics professor at Cambridge University. No doubt, today, critics would cite super-ESP as their explanation.

'Most mediums are nowadays classed as "mental mediums".'

121

other source, this would be regarded as 'evidential'. However, proving that the information is known only to the deceased and the person who receives it (preferably after some research) is very difficult.

Since researchers coined the term 'super-ESP' it has been necessary to apply a strict system to research on survival. According to this theory, if a fact is recorded anywhere at all, the medium's mind can travel to that place to find the information and repeat it at a sitting. They may be able to read the sitter's mind, enter a locked room and read the contents of a sealed envelope, or even consult some such source as the 'Akashic record', a cosmic data bank in which all facts that have ever been known and events that have ever taken place are said to be recorded.

Sensible researchers reject the idea of using one unproven phenomenon to disprove another. Rather than trying to provide incontestable evidence of survival that even the most hostile critic cannot object to, an altogether more productive approach is to amass case material that is based on well-planned research and is suggestive of survival. If the results are then analysed objectively for 'veridicality' (how strong the evidence is), such a body of cases can be quite convincing.

' ... the most obvious place to start is to seek out the services of a reliable medium.'

• HOW TO COLLECT EVIDENCE •

Assessing information for and against survival will be the same whether you are conducting a case investigation or carrying out research on your own behalf. For your own projects, the most obvious place to start is to seek out the services of a reliable medium. In a case, this stage will have been completed before your involvement.

Mediums have existed for a long time. The western world largely lost its knowledge of ancient spiritual practices such as shamanism in the wake of Christianity, but some elements remained among practitioners of the old religions. Mediums came to be in demand in the mid-1800s, a time of social upheaval and spiritual renewal, when spiritualism took off in the United States (see 'Strange Rapping Noises', page 129).

The casual researcher will not generally witness physical mediumship these days, apart from occasional demonstrations of transfiguration. Many researchers bent on exposing fraud have criticised this phenomenon, the most infamous case being that of Helen Duncan, prosecuted under the United Kingdom's Witchcraft Act of 1735 during the Second World War (see right).

Many classic Victorian materialisation cases have been re-examined and found lacking in evidence, despite the involvement of the leading scientists of the day. The desire to believe seems to have misled many of them. One of the most frequently quoted cases involved chemist

PROSECUTED FOR WITCHCRAFT

During the Second World War, Scottish medium Helen Duncan fell foul of the 1735 Witchcraft Act, which made it illegal to falsely claim to have psychic powers. Helen had been active as a medium for many years and had a faithful following. Her speciality was the production of materializations clad in 'ectoplasm', described as muslin-like, sometimes almost transparent, usually white and often having an unpleasant aroma.

Helen allowed intimate physical examinations by researchers, particularly in the earlier part of her career. Many people attending the medium's séances were convinced that they had been reunited with loved ones, claiming to have recognized voices, faces, accents and patterns of speech.

Helen Duncan's downfall came during her frequent stays in Portsmouth. This naval port was a busy base for wartime operations, and there were many people in the city waiting for news of loved ones. At one séance in 1943 a sailor had reportedly communicated the fact of his death long before it was officially announced that his ship had gone down.

In January 1944 a disbeliever, a Naval lieutenant, took the chance he was looking for to stop Mrs Duncan by exposing her as a fraud. He arranged for a police officer to pounce on her at a séance and grab samples of ecto-plasm. Although nothing incriminating was retrieved at the time of her arrest, she later appeared at the Old Bailey in London, accused of pretending to be a medium. She was sent to Holloway prison in London, where she spent nine months. She continued to work after her release, but became ill in 1956 following a police raid on a séance in Nottingham. They were said to be looking for beards, masks and shrouds but seemingly came away empty-handed. She never recovered from the shock, and died five weeks later.

Recent reviewers of these events who are campaigning for Helen Duncan's pardon believe she was imprisoned because of her success in passing on messages before news had been released by the Admiralty. This could have been bad for the country's morale. The Navy also feared that the secret details of the D-Day landings could have got into the wrong hands. The controversy continues …

The Criticisms

• Amounts of muslin could be hidden in the body's orifices, not just the stomach. The 'ectoplasm' would then be regurgitated or extracted during the séance and formed into body-like shapes.

• Photographs show vague shapes, usually with a strange, two-dimensional head attached at the top. It was often alleged that these were just papier mâché heads or paper cutouts attached to cheesecloth.

123

William Crookes, who investigated medium Florence Cook and the materialized figure of 'Katie King'. Contemporary scientific techniques did not permit foolproof controls, and one look at early photographs of materializations is enough to convince not only sceptics but also most reasonable people of their fraudulent nature.

Most mediums are nowadays classed as 'mental mediums'. Many operate through spiritualist churches or give demonstrations to the general public in concert halls. Others can be found at psychic fairs or even through newspaper advertisements. Ask around, too, as it is surprising just how many colleagues or friends will have visited or heard of a local medium.

EXPERIMENTS WITH MEDIUMS

• Contact several psychic artists at the same time to compare the portraits they produce. How many spirit guides do they come up with? Assess any written messages they send with the portraits. See if they agree on any points.

• Contact several mediums for postal readings – either tapes or written readings. Assess the messages and look for similar summaries of your current situation. Check for any predictions, and record if and when these events happen.

• Arrange a series of sittings with a medium and take along in a sealed container an object belonging to a deceased person (friend, relative or person unknown to you) and see if that elicits any relevant messages. Ensure that the object cannot be discerned in any way through the container, for example, by shaking or prodding it. To vary the proceedings, either conceal the object about your person and do not refer to it, or mention that you would like to try an experiment if the medium does not object and put the container on the table. Allow the medium to handle the container and use psychometry to establish contact.

• Take the object from the last point to a series of different mediums and compare the results.

• VISITING A MEDIUM •

Once you have found a medium, the way they prefer to practise will largely dictate how your research will be conducted. If you choose a demonstration of clairvoyance at a spiritualist church as your initial approach, you will have to wait patiently to see if the medium comes to you with a message. The same goes for public demonstrations, where the size of the audience means the odds are against your being spoken to. However, both can act as a forum for gathering information on how mediums work and the type of message that is likely to be conveyed.

'If you can arrange a private sitting so much the better.'

A PRIVATE SITTING

If you can arrange a private sitting, so much the better. Mediums working within the spiritualist churches will be keen to provide good evidence for you, including names and dates. Psychics working at fairs may not be spiritualists, but their methods of working are largely similar – sometimes they use tarot cards, runes or other prompts to aid their work.

When you go to the sitting take along:

◈ A notepad, or ask the medium's permission to use a portable cassette recorder, as you will find it difficult to remember all that is said.

◈ Guard against supplying any information during the sitting. It is not in your interest or the medium's.

◈ Many mediums will explain to you how the sitting will be conducted and advise you how to respond to them.

◈ Be wary of mediums who ask for information – they are either not particularly good, not on form that day, or just fraudulent.

◈ Most mediums will ask questions, as they can need voice contact from you to help the flow of messages.

◈ Try to answer without giving yourself away. A simple 'yes' or 'no', 'I can accept that' or 'I can't place that' will do.

' … any medium can be expected to pick up clues fairly accurately.'

THE CHAFFIN WILL AFFAIR

This classic case was first reported in the 1920s and shows how the deceased wanted to contact with the living world. Mr Chaffin died in 1921, and his 1905 will gave the bulk of his estate to his third son, which left the rest of the family virtually penniless.

In 1921 Mr Chaffin appeared at the bedside of one of his disinherited sons. He was recognizable through the old overcoat he had often worn when alive. When he appeared on a second occasion the apparition spoke, telling the son to search for his will in the pocket of the overcoat. When they searched the coat, which was then in the possession of another son, they found a note sewn into its lining which referred to a bible originally owned by Mr Chaffin's father. This bible had been kept by Mrs Chaffin. It was opened in the presence of witnesses

and another will fell out. It was dated 1919 and divided Mr Chaffin's estate in equal portions. Mr Chaffin then appeared a third time, after the will had been found, seemingly still concerned about the injustice done to his family.

The chain of events involved represents a good case for survival:

• As summed up by the late author and researcher, D. Scott Rogo, even the super-ESP theory can be discounted.

• What the apparition said was not strictly true: the will was actually in the bible, not the pocket or coat lining.

• No one but the late Mr Chaffin had known the whole story, and the pieces had to be put together by the various members of the family following the clues to find the answer.

◈ Even if you manage not to give away facts by speaking out, your body language can reveal a lot of information about your acceptance of the messages. Mediums are often described as 'sensitives', and any medium can be expected to pick up clues fairly accurately.

THE LENGTH OF A SITTING

Generally, you will have about half an hour to an hour's worth of messages, or predictions, to analyze afterwards. A good method of assessing how successful a sitting was is to write up your notes, or transcribe the tape recording, separating and evaluate every piece of information (see right). Discount any statements that were prompted by something you said.

Write a comment alongside to explain why you accept or reject a statement. Give each a mark for 'veridicality' on a scale from one to ten: mark 0 for totally irrelevant, five for so-so and 10 for evidential. If you apply the same scale to each sitting, you will soon build up not only experience of evaluation, but also a body of evidence that can be subjected to objective examination by others. Your assessment will also be enhanced by a working knowledge of statistics.

• PLANNING A PROJECT WITH A MEDIUM •

Once you have gained experience of how mediums work you can start to plan your research. Maybe you have built up a good relationship with a particular medium who is interested in your project. Obviously by now the medium will know quite a lot about you. The messages assessed should not, therefore, repeat information already established as part of your own 'history'. If there is no one medium you wish to work with, your project could try to get information from a group of unrelated mediums, perhaps using different techniques, over a certain period of time, for the purpose of comparison (see 'Experiments with Mediums', page 124).

• EVALUATING A SITTING •

Not all messages can be assessed fully. Often the message does not identify the communicator clearly. Some will be impossible to check out, particularly if they involve obscure family history or refer to a person's confidential medical history. Certain common situations will crop up, such as the sitter being presented with a bunch of flowers, or a communicator who comes through with a hacking cough. While the

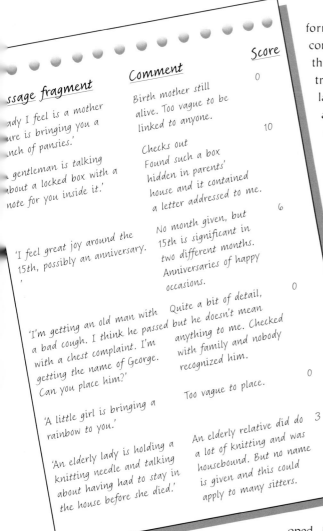

...ssage fragment	Comment	Score
...ady I feel is a mother ...ure is bringing you a ...nch of pansies.'	Birth mother still alive. Too vague to be linked to anyone.	0
...gentleman is talking ...bout a locked box with a note for you inside it.'	Checks out Found such a box hidden in parents' house and it contained a letter addressed to me.	10
'I feel great joy around the 15th, possibly an anniversary.'	No month given, but 15th is significant in two different months. Anniversaries of happy occasions.	6
'I'm getting an old man with a bad cough. I think he passed with a chest complaint. I'm getting the name of George. Can you place him?'	Quite a bit of detail, but he doesn't mean anything to me. Checked with family and nobody recognized him.	0
'A little girl is bringing a rainbow to you.'	Too vague to place.	0
'An elderly lady is holding a knitting needle and talking about having had to stay in the house before she died.'	An elderly relative did do a lot of knitting and was housebound. But no name is given and this could apply to many sitters.	3

former is an artefact of the communication process, reflecting the imagery used in receiving and transmitting the message, the latter image is intended to show a 'life condition' that may have contributed to the communicator's passing.

The box opposite shows an example of how to assess typical messages. How would you score them?

· PROJECTS · WITHOUT A MEDIUM

If you do not wish to use mediums, a number of options for research projects still remain open. The results, as always, are unpredictable and can be disappointing. It is often suggested that everyone has hidden spiritual talents just waiting to be developed. Many spiritualist churches offer development circles to serious students, but if you are not certain of your beliefs you may want to tap your talents some other way.

AUTOMATIC WRITING

This has a fairly reputable history. Archeologist Frederick Bligh Bond discovered lost knowledge of the ruined site of the Benedictine Abbey of St Mary, Glastonbury, through messages purporting to come from monks who lived around the time of the monastery's construction. Subsequent excavations proved the messages to be correct. Matthew Manning, a British psychic and healer, experienced automatic writing in his home during his teenage years. This was largely composed of signatures appearing on his bedroom walls when the room was empty, and various writings produced through Matthew's hand, but which claimed to come from discarnate entities including one Robert Webbe. The Surrealists led by André Breton used this technique in the 1920s: phrases tumbling onto the paper from their subconscious minds were used as a way to generate creative writing. There is, therefore, no guarantee that any messages written down are in fact coming from the next world.

◇ PRACTISING AUTOMATIC WRITING

You should sit with a pen and paper and clear your mind. Let your hand write whatever comes, whether scribblings or a recognizable script. If you can subsequently read what you have written, copy it out and submit it to the same analytic approach as set out above. You may, of course, have produced nonsense. If automatic writing does not occur spontaneously, it can take time to develop and boredom can set in quickly.

A word of warning is appropriate here. With techniques like automatic writing you should always be aware of psychological dangers. Many people will doubtless have experimented with Ouija boards in their youth. Inevitably, sensational messages emerged purporting to be from entities claiming to be 'the devil' or similar. While these were probably the result of deliberate pushing by excited youngsters, disturbing messages can sometimes emerge from such sources as automatic writing. If you do not like the possibility of being exposed to such content then don't attempt it.

HYPNOTIC REGRESSION

This procedure is often quoted as a way of providing definite evidence of past lives, and therefore survival. However, when the information is examined objectively it is usually found to be wanting. If you want to try out hypnotic regression, ensure that you visit a reputable hypnotist. There are dangers inherent in this field, and a number of well-known hypnotists have found themselves in court in recent years accused of carelessness and neglecting the physical and mental wellbeing of people they have worked with, primarily when acting as stage hypnotists.

◇ THE FLY-PAPER THEORY

This theory may account for the past-life experience and therefore bears closer examination. It was devised by researchers taking part in a hypnotic regression project led by Dr Hugh Pincott, a paranormal researcher, in the mid-1980s.

Hugh Pincott proposes that there is possibly within each of us a latent personality which is our unconscious desire and ambition for ourselves. This could lie completely dormant for most of a person's life-time but, like a fly-paper, can draw to itself those facts and experiences gleaned from the vast reservoir of daily experience. This can then flesh out the skeleton which could pop out as a full character when the circumstances are favourable – as in deep hypnosis. A bus conductor may see himself as a deep-sea explorer, a drudge-ridden housewife as queen Boadicea, or a company accountant as an engine driver. These ambitions may have been denied to each person on account of background, upbringing or necessity.

Dr Pincott points out that no single theory can account fully for observations, otherwise we would use stronger terms such as 'explanations' or 'answers'. One profitable way to proceed is not to overlook the possibility that more than one may be invoked, at various times, to account for the material provided by a subject. In the case where the spoken material is of an exceptionally high quality, and intensive historical research has ruled out, in turn, hoaxing, fantasy and cryptomnesia, we are left with a few strong contenders. These include the cosmic data bank, survival of death and genuine past lives. Perhaps they are all just one and the same, or at least different aspects of the same idea.

STRANGE RAPPING NOISES

• *In March 1848 the tenants of a house in upstate New York experienced unexplained rapping noises. Kate Fox, the youngest daughter of the household, reportedly established communication with a 'spirit' by means of a code which allowed questions to be answered by a specified number of raps. The raps revealed that the responses were coming from a man who had been murdered in the house and buried in the cellar. Later questioning, involving the neighbours, revealed his identity as Charles B. Rosma, who had had his throat cut and been robbed of $500, five years earlier. In 1904, a skeleton was found in the walls of the house.*

• THE ORIGINS OF • SPIRITUALISM

Reports of spiritual activities or odd happenings that occurred in the late 19th century soon spread, and spirit communications at sittings took off. Within a few years the number of practising mediums had greatly increased, and tours to Europe were organized. It was not long before physical phenomena such as table turning became very popular in Victorian society. From these beginnings, at times frivolous, dubious or fraudulent, came spiritualism and a much more serious approach. Although the religion now has legal status in the United Kingdom, it is still misunderstood by many non-believers.

PREMONITIONS

FORESEEING
THE FUTURE

E VERYONE EXPERIENCES PREMONITIONS in their lifetime. Ask almost any friend or relative and they will almost certainly say that they have 'known' that something was going to happen before it did. Indeed, if you look into your past it is very likely that you too will have experienced just such an event. Maybe you knew when someone was about to phone you or you had a nasty feeling about some future event and something untoward did indeed happen. Or perhaps you dreamed correctly what would happen to you the next day.

The definition of a premonition is simply foretelling the future. Obviously we can predict normal routine, everyday events, but a premonition must be something more. It must be an event we predict that is beyond everyday expectation or current trends. You could predict that an earthquake may occur in a vulnerable zone such as California. To say one was going to happen in the next few years is scarcely a premonition, but if you predicted one in the next few days, when seismologists have said it is unlikely, then that IS a premonition.

'The definition of a premonition is simply foretelling the future.'

• THE SCIENTIFIC VIEW •

Premonitions are classified as 'precognition' by scientists. They are the apparent ability to predict the future beyond the expectations of chance. Experiments devised to test these abilities include such things as predicting the turn of cards or dice that have yet to be moved (see Chapter 8, 'Are You Psychic?'). Although certain scientists study the subject, many more see no point in even trying. This is because they support the common-sense view that predicting the future is impossible. It is believed that time can play strange tricks in physics in the microscopic world of atomic particles and the huge scale of galaxies, but few believe it can do so in our everyday world.

Even non-scientists can readily see the obvious flaw in being able to tell the future. If we can predict the future we can also change it. In doing so our prediction is invalidated. This causes problems for scientific theories just as much as it defies common sense. Most scientists see time as a one-way path along which we travel, never to return or jump ahead. Attempts to integrate precognition into science seem doomed to failure. But persistent reports of people experiencing precognition appear regularly. If these could be proven with very good evidence, then the scientists would have to change their world view drastically.

'Premonitions are classified as "precognition" by scientists.'

• INVESTIGATING PREMONITIONS •

As with other phenomena the first priority is to gather together all the facts. As in other fields of the paranormal, witnesses are often quick to draw conclusions that do not stand up to intense scrutiny. There is an understandable desire for the fantastic or extraordinary to be true. Sadly, often it is not. With premonitions there are three things to consider:

◇ Did the event take place as reported.

◇ Was it really predicted.

◇ What were the chances of it being predicted?

The first two parts of this exercise involve investigative techniques discussed in Chapter 1, 'Investigating'. The third part requires a basic appreciation of the laws of chance.

The main aim of investigating premonitions is to provide scientifically useful evidence. You need to analyze what would convince scientists that people can really see into the future. The theory to beat, from a scientific viewpoint, is coincidence. It is obviously possible that a person just happened to think of an event just before it occurred.

Most of us now live to a reasonable age, so we must occasionally happen to guess the future correctly. Indeed, if we have a mathematical chance of, say, one in ten thousand of guessing some future event correctly, then if we kept trying all our lives it would be almost inevitable that we would do so at least once. Indeed, statistically speaking, it would be odd if we did not guess correctly once in a while. And yet odds of ten thousand to one sound incredibly impressive. But over a sufficiently long time interval such an unlikely event is almost inevitable.

Consider another example. What are the chances of one person dreaming about someone they have not met for a long time and then unexpectedly meeting them the next day? Quite low, as you might

131

imagine. But if you consider the 250 million people living in a country like the USA, and then think about the chances of this happening to at least a few of these on any one night the number of incidences are a lot higher, as you might imagine. People this happens to will no doubt be amazed, but it is the sheer number of people involved that makes an event such as this almost inevitable.

'Most premonitions are only noticed after the predicted event has taken place'

A further statistical point to consider is this: how often are you convinced that something is going to happen and then it doesn't? These failures are probably not remembered. Scientifically speaking, we ought to but probably won't. If we have one success in predicting an event, then this has to be weighed against the dozens of failures in order to be put into true perspective.

So in assessing a claim of a premonition the important thing is to work out just how unlikely it really is. Sadly, even if it is incredibly unlikely there is still no real mathematical reason why we should not manage premonitions occasionally. If we regularly foretell the future against high odds, however, it may begin to become convincing scientifically. The other important point (as with all anomalous phenomena) is to establish that the event really happened as described. Anyone can claim that they predicted something once it has happened. To be convincing, they need to record their prediction in detail in advance.

• TYPES OF PREMONITION •

Most premonitions are only noticed after the predicted event has taken place. Most of us have no witnesses and we alone know we were right.

Another rarer kind of premonition is one that is accompanied by a definite feeling of significance:

❖ You may get a foreboding that something awful is going to happen.

❖ A striking dream may be experienced about an extremely unusual subject.

❖ Or, if you are used to premonitions, you might simply recognize a new one from previous experience. If you, or anyone you know, is lucky enough to be in this situation, do record it in advance, with a premonitions bureau.

PREMONITIONS BUREAUX

The way such bureaux work is simplicity itself. If someone feels they have had a premonition, they record the fact in writing and send it to the

THE CASE OF THE LONG-EARED OWL

A report related to a paranormal researcher concerned a woman called Jill, an avid birdwatcher. One night, Jill dreamt that she caught a bus into the countryside on a Friday evening. She took a seat behind two men she knew, one of whom said he made that particular journey regularly. Later in the dream the three of them were walking along a country lane with several other people. Jill was carrying a pair of binoculars with her and spotted a long-eared owl sitting very still on a stone garden ornament. She pointed this sighting out to her companions, explaining how unusual it was to see such a rare bird. She also saw two kingfishers that were perched in a nearby tree, and showed her companions these too. Then the dream ended.

Next morning Jill and her boyfriend set out to go birdwatching, as they had done regularly for many years. She told him about her dream and he joked that seeing a long-eared owl was about the last thing that could happen that day. They were travelling to try and see an American bittern, a rare bird in the north of England. But, when they arrived they were astounded to see a long-eared owl (the first they had ever seen), as well as the expected bittern. Long-eared owls are rarely seen by bird-watchers as they are highly nocturnal and usually live away from built-up areas. Jill had been trying to see one for years without success and had never dreamed of seeing one before.

Although most of the events in the dream Jill reported did not come true, and could not reasonably be expected to, the climax – sighting the owl – does match the chief event of the following day.

Unfortunately, she did not write up an account of her dream before the real event with the owl took place.

Analysis of case study

You need to examine what sort of things should be done to establish whether this case was really a premonition. The main points to establish are: how unlikely the predicted event is and whether you can verify that the prediction actually occurred at the time stated. So in relation to the case study detailed you would have needed to ask the following questions:

• Was the dream recorded in writing before the apparent fulfilment?
• This event was witnessed by Jill's boyfriend but, as no written record was made, for details both their memories are being relied on.
• Find out how often Jill remembers her dreams. She may recall many dreams; some people, however, do not even remember their dreams at all so their chances of getting a premonition this way would be remote.
• Discover how often Jill predicts anything correctly. She may not have had many premonitions, so this could just be a one-off incident.
• You need to work out how much of the dream came true as clearly some of it was fantasy. The more that is remembered the larger the pool of material is from which to draw coincidences.
• Try and work out the likelihood of that particular owl being at that site. Owls often visit the same sites to roost every night, so anyone who knew the site would have easily predicted they might be there.
• Find out if the birdwatchers would have known this information in advance as they did actually live a long distance away.
• Overall: a good prediction but everyone gets a few in a lifetime.

bureau. A letter date-stamped by the post office might be considered sufficient. There are obvious problems with this, of course. A letter could be opened and the contents altered before being resealed. Obviously, this depends very much on the integrity of the people operating the bureau. Sometimes a form is used that records all the details all about your premonition before the event takes place, then presuming it does happen a fulfilment form is filled out to identify the elements of the reported premonition.

'You may get a foreboding that something awful is going to happen'

Once the fulfilment form is received the premonition will be judged against several factors:

◇ Firstly there is accuracy. The more facts that are correct (time, place, precise order of events and the people involved) the higher the score.

◇ Secondly there is the likelihood of the event. If something is so obvious that any intelligent, informed person could have guessed what would happen that will not score highly.

◇ Thirdly is how closely the person is involved with the event themselves. For instance, if the event involves a family relative, it would not score as highly as an unexpected political development on the other side of the world. Any way of objectively backing up the premonition, such as a press clipping or sworn statement from a witness, would be very helpful.

In recent years, the inception of email has meant there are new methods of collecting predictions. Email is also date stamped by its carrier. It can, moreover, be copied unread to any number of third parties on receipt. These third parties could simply keep the mail until they believe the prediction has come true. Having so many copies in existence reduces the chance of any tampering. For such reasons it is probably the way forward for such bureaux.

• INVESTIGATING TIMESLIPS •

Timeslips, such as detailed in the case study opposite, are when a person or persons experience an incident that seems to be set in the past. So, how do you go about investigating such a report? Essentially, such cases can be treated in the same way as reports of ghosts (see Chapter 1, 'Investigating' and Chapter 2, 'Hauntings'). However, it is particularly important in timeslip cases to bear the following points in mind:

! DREAM PREMONITION

J. W. Dunne was serving in the Boer War in the spring of 1902 when he had a vivid dream. He dreamt that he was standing on a volcanic mountain situated on an island. He had dreamt of the island before and just knew that it was threatened by a volcanic eruption. He felt terrified and felt impelled to try and save the 4,000 islanders. He desperately tried to get French officials on a neighbouring island to get ships ready to help with the aftermath of the . impending disaster. The dream then took on a nightmare quality as he seemed to be rushing against time but getting nowhere, and constantly heard the message that 4,000 people would die unless he helped.

A few days later Dunne received a copy of the *Daily Telegraph* and he was immediately drawn to the headline:

Volcano disaster in Martinique
Possible loss of over 40,000 lives

The dream was slightly strange as it could not be termed a premonition as it took place just after the tragedy occurred when the newspaper was already on its way to him. While reading the article he misread the number of lives lost as 4,000 instead of 40,000 and this became fixed in his mind and whenever he related his dream he also said the same wrong figure. He later discovered his mistake, but his unconscious mind in his dream had also made the same mistake.

From *An Experiment with Time*, New York 1938

◇ HISTORY
Check the history of the site. Just because someone has witnessed a scene from history, it does not automatically mean it must be accurate.

◇ RESEARCH
Find out all you can from maps, plans, photographs and historical records. The first thing to establish is when the historical scene is likely to have taken place. A reported timeslip in the early 1950s, for example, was of battle sounds heard by two women at a site in Dieppe near to a massive allied raid which occurred some nine years earlier. They purported to have no knowledge of the nearby battle at the time of the incident.

◇ WITNESSES
Establish how much the witness knew of the history of the area. Make sure your study of the site is very thorough. Sometimes you may find things that are not recorded in official histories but nevertheless might have been present at the apparent 'time' seen by the witness.

'Timeslips are so rare that it seems fairly pointless to stage a vigil.'

135

THE CASE OF THE VILLAGE TIMESLIP

Timeslips are rare occurrences but this one was recorded by paranormal researcher Melanie Warren.

The incident happened over 20 years ago, in a village in England, when Angela (pseudonym) was 15, but it's something she will never forget as the incident was so vivid and no logical explanation has been found for what happened.

One day during her holidays, Angela offered to take two young girls to meet their mother, who worked at the nearby Lakeview Hotel and take Tiger, the dog for a walk at the same time. It was late autumn and dark, and as Angela and the girls walked down a little back lane that leads to the Lakeview, Angela began to feel strange. The thought that came into her head was 'this is a bad night'.

She dropped the girls off at the Lakeview, but took a different route home, going past the hotel, the churchyard, and then back home along the main road. As she was passing the churchyard, a very tall gentleman wearing an old-fashioned black coat with a cape passed her, and Angela immediately felt sorry for him because he looked ill.

As he passed her, Tiger strained at her leash trying to follow the man. Angela pulled the struggling dog and when she tried to pick her up, the dog snapped at her, which was totally out of character.

While struggling with the dog, Angela noticed the man approach a large three storey house and walk up the steps and go in the front door. She also saw that a maid came to the door wearing a long dress, mob cap and a frilly apron.

Tiger was still straining at her lead, so Angela finally picked her up (by the scruff of the neck) to get her home. Once home Angela told her story to her parents. But as she related the details, she suddenly realized that the man had walked into a house that wasn't there.

Angela was now seriously unsettled and wanted to go back to the churchyard, to check out what she'd seen. Her father went with her, and they went straight to the place where she had seen the house. But when she looked again all she saw was the Lakeview Hotel's large lounge window.

A few years later, Angela's father brought her a booklet of local ghost stories. And discovered that she wasn't the only one to have had a strange experience in the same vicinity as the Lakeview and the church. One point that Angela was most puzzled by was that the building she saw – a large house – bore no resemblance to the present hotel. But on investigation it was discovered that the hotel had originally been a large Georgian house which had been demolished to make way for the present hotel.

' … the first thing to establish is whether the events really happened the way they were reported.'

Timeslips are so rare that it seems fairly pointless to stage a vigil. Often they are only reported to happen once or are possibly repeated after intervals of several years. Often the best you can do is interview witnesses and examine the scene and then try to find out if anyone else has experienced anything similar. If they have, check to see if the details seem to match. Timeslip cases are very rare but well worth the effort because of their scientific significance.

• BACK IN TIME •

This Lakeview Hotel account (left), if taken at face value, appears to be an example of retrocognition. This means witnessing events from the past in the present. But ghosts often seem to inhabit a time gone by, following old building layouts in their wanderings. So how is retrocognition different? Another way of looking at such experiences is as a timeslip. Instead of a ghost, which we could view as a character from another time walking through our present day world, it is as though we have physically slipped back in time into theirs.

It could also be a special case of a recording-type ghost in which a whole scene is replayed instead of just an isolated figure. However, the first thing to establish is whether the events really happened the way they were reported.

There have been several reported cases of this type. Indeed, there are enough to suggest that we may be dealing with a genuine phenomenon. As discussed earlier, there are celebrated cases of people apparently witnessing historic battles. In the best known timeslip case, that of one witnessed at Versailles, two women wandered around what seemed to be a complete scene from the past for hours.

FURTHER READING

HAUNTINGS AND POLTERGEISTS

Alan Gauld and A.D. Cornell, **Poltergeists**, Routledge & Kegan Paul, 1979

Andrew MacKenzie, **Hauntings and Apparitions**, Heinemann, 1982

Guy Lyon Playfair, **This House is Haunted**, Souvenir Press, 1980

William G. Roll, **The Poltergeist**, Scarecrow Press, 1976

John Spencer and Tony Wells, **Ghost Watching**, Virgin Books, 1994

Peter Underwood, **The Ghost-Hunter's Guide**, Blandford Press, 1986

UFOs

Paul Devereux and Peter Brookesmith, **Ufos and Ufology**, Blandford, 1998

Hilary Evans, **Visions, Apparitions, Alien Visitors**, Thorsons, 1984

Carl Jung, **Flying Saucers - a Modern Myth**, RKP, 1959

John Spencer, **The New UFO Encyclopaedia**, Headline, 1997

FORTEAN PHENOMENA

Janet and Colin Bord, **Alien Animals**, Panther, 1985

William R. Corliss, **The Sourcebook Project** - a series of books cataloguing Fortean phenomena: contact The Sourcebook Project, P.O. Box 107, Glen Arm, MD 21057, USA

Mike Dash, **Borderlands**, Heinemann, 1997

John Michell and Robert J.M. Rickard, **Phenomena**, Thames and Hudson, 1977

EARTH MYSTERIES

Julian Cope, **The Modern Antiquarian**, Thorsons, 199

Paul Devereux and Ian Thompson, **The Ley Guide**, Empress, 1987

Tom Graves, **The Diviners Handbook**, Aquarian, 198

Philip Heselton, **The Elements of Earth Mysteries**, Element, 1991

John Michell, **The New View over Atlantis**, Thames and Hudson, 1983

Guy Underwood, **The Pattern of the Past**, Abacus, 1972

Alfred Watkins, **The Old Straight Track**, Abacus, 1974

MOTE VIEWING

ichael Bentine, **Doors of the Mind**, Grafton 1984

seph McMoneagle, **Mind Trek**, Hampton Roads 1997

n Schnabel, **Remote Viewers: Secret History America's Psychic Spies**, Dell 1997

ssell Targ & Keith Harary, **The Mind Race**, w English Library 1985

OINCIDENCES

hn William Dunne, **An Experiment with Time**, ndon 1927 (with several later reprints)

r Alister Hardy, Robert Harvie and Arthur Koestler, he Challenge of Chance, Hutchinson, London, 1973

ian Inglis, **Coincidence**, Hutchinson, London 1990

rthur Koestler, **Arrow in the Blue**, 1952

nny Randles, **Beyond Explanation**, London 1985

P, PK AND PREMONITIONS

ichard Broughton, **Parapsychology**, Rider, 1991

ans J. Eysenck and Carl Sargent, **Explaining the nexplained**, Weidenfeld and Nicolson, 1983

hn Hasted, **The Metal-Benders**, outledge & Kegan-Paul, 1981

L. Randall, **Parapsychology and the Nature of Life**, ouvenir, 1974

ana Zohar, **Through the Time Barrier**, einemann, 1982

OUT-OF-THE-BODY EXPERIENCES

S. Blackmore, **Beyond the Body: An Investigation of Out-of-the-Body Experiences**, Paladin, 1982

H. Irwin, **Flight of Mind: A Psychological Study of the Out-of-Body Experience**, Scarecrow Press, 1985

R. Monroe, **Journeys Out of the Body**, Doubleday, 1971

S. Muldoon and H. Carrington, **The Projection of the Astral Body**, Rider & Co, 1929

NEAR-DEATH EXPERIENCE

S. Blackmore, **Dying to Live - Near-Death Experiences**, Prometheus Books, 1993

D. Darling, **Afterlife**, 4th Estate, 1995

R. Moody, **Life After Life**, Mockingbird, 1975

K. Osis and E. Haraldsson, **At the Hour of Death.** Avon, 1977

K. Ring, **Life at Death - A Scientific Investigation of the Near-Death Experience**, Coward, McCann and Geoghegan, 1980

LIFE AFTER DEATH

Anon., **Hints on Sitting with Mediums**, SPR, revised edition 1965

Frederick Bligh Bond, **The Gate of Remembrance**, Blackwell, 1918

Manfred Cassirer, **Medium on Trial: The Story of Helen Duncan and the Witchcraft Act**, PN Publishing, 1996

Paul Deane, **How to Contact the Dead**, Atlantis, 1998

D. Scott Rogo, **Life After Death: The Case for Survival of Bodily Death**, Aquarian, 1986

GLOSSARY

APPARITIONS – the unexplained appearance of a person, animal or object.

ASTROLOGY – divination through celestial bodies.

AUTOMATIC WRITING – the ability to transfer messages or thoughts from spirits in the form of written messages.

CLAIRVOYANCE – the apparent ability to see not using the physical eyes.

DOWSING – to divine or search for information beyond the capability of the five normal senses.

EXTRA-SENSORY PERCEPTION – obtaining information in some way other than five normal senses.

FALLS FROM THE SKY – unusual or unexplained objects.

FIREWALKING – walking barefoot over hot coals without ill effect.

GLOSSOLALIA – speaking in tongues with no recognizable language.

HAUNTING – a visitation in the form of a ghost or poltergeist.

HEALING (UNORTHODOX) – huge subject encompassing all kinds of alternative and psychic medicine.

HYPERAESTHESIA – unusual heightening of the normal senses.

HYPNOSIS – artificially induced state of relaxation in which deeper parts of the mind become accessible.

HYPNOTIC REGRESSION – use of hypnosis to recall information about the past.

INCORRUPTIBILITY – corpses that do not decay naturally.

LEVITATION – the ability to rise and float in the air.

LEY LINES – a line joining points in the landscape following an ancient track.

MATERIALIZATION – deliberately contrived appearance of dead human figures.

MEDIUMSHIP – a spiritual intermediary between the dead and the living.

METAL BENDING – ability to bend metal objects through the use of physic power.

MULTIPLE PERSONALITY – people displaying personalities with no knowledge of each other.

MYSTERY ANIMAL – unexplained appearance of an animal outside its natural habitat.

OUT-OF-THE-BODY EXPERIENCE – feeling of being detached from one's body and ability to observe surrounding environment.

POLTERGEIST - manifestation of an apparition or presence involving noises and physical movement of objects.

POSSESSION – control of a living being by a non-corporeal entity (for example 'spirit').

PRECOGNITION – ability to forsee the future.

PSYCHOKINESIS – the apparent ability of a person to influence or alter their environment physically without direct or indirect contact.

PSYCHOMETRY – the measurement and testing of psychic abilities.

REINCARNATION – transmigration of a 'soul' from one body at death to be born into another.

SPIRITUALISM – belief that spirits of the dead can communicate with the living.

SPONTANEOUS HUMAN COMBUSTION – humans burning without source of ignition.

TELEPATHY – ability to read or receive another person's thoughts.

TELEPORTATION – abnormal disappearance of object followed by reappearance elsewhere.

TELAESTHESIA – perceiving distant objects without conventional sensory contact.

UNIDENTIFIED FLYING OBJECTS – unexplained objects witnessed in the sky.

VISIONS – a mystical or religious experience of seeing an event or person.

XENOGLOSSIA – speaking in tongues with a recognized language that is foreign to the speaker.

INDEX

· ORGANIZATIONS ·

Association for the Scientific Study of Anomalous Phenomena
(ASSAP), 20 Paul Street, Frome, Somerset, BA11 1DX, UK

British UFO Research Association (BUFORA),
16 Southway, Burgess Hill, Sussex RH15 9ST, UK

Society for Psychical Research (SPR),
49 Marloes Road, Kensington, London W8 6LA, UK

Parapsychology Foundation Inc.,
228 East 71st Street, New York, NY 10021

The American Society for Psychical Research (ASPR),
4 West 73rd Street, New York, NY 10021

· ACKNOWLEDGEMENTS ·

Alan Cleaver (*table-tilting, big cat sighting*)
Adam Bailey (*premonition case*)
Melanie Warren (*timeslip case*)
Robin Laurence (*Dover Castle case*)
Michael Lewis (*vigil organization*)
David Thomas (*Blue Bell Hill case*)
Chris Walton (*investigation checklists*)
Simon Earwicker (*photography hints*)
All at ASSAP

Various chapter authors also contributed material to chapters
other than their own.

The Publishers would like to thank Mary Lambert, Janet Swarbrick and
Marie Lorimer for all their help.

· PICTURE CREDITS ·